Hobart Paperback No. 24

KEYNES'S *GENERAL THEORY*:
FIFTY YEARS ON

D1344890

"THE FELLER OUGHT TO BE ASHAMED! ENCOURAGING RAIN!"

Cartoon by David Low (first published in *The Evening Standard*, 5 January 1938) : by
permission of *The London Evening Standard*.

Keynes's *General Theory*: Fifty Years On

Its Relevance and Irrelevance to Modern Times

John Burton · Leland B. Yeager

Milton Friedman · Karl Brunner

Michael R. Darby and James R. Lothian

Alan A. Walters · Patrick Minford

Michael Beenstock · Alan Budd

Published by
THE INSTITUTE OF ECONOMIC AFFAIRS
1986

First published in December 1986
by
The Institute of Economic Affairs
2 Lord North Street,
Westminster, London SW1P 3LB

© The Institute of Economic Affairs 1986

ISSN 0309-1783

ISBN 0-255 36197-1

Printed in Great Britain by
GORON PRO-PRINT CO LTD,
CHURCHILL INDUSTRIAL ESTATE, LANCING, WEST SUSSEX
Set in 'Monotype' Baskerville

Contents

ILLUSTRATIONS

J. M. Keynes drawn by David Low (first published in the *New Statesman & Nation*, 28 October 1933): by permission of *The London Evening Standard*.

Photograph of J. M. Keynes (*Picture Post*, 10 November 1945): by permission of BBC Hulton Picture Library.

Introductory Essay

Fifty Years On:
Background and Foreground

JOHN BURTON

Research Director,
Institute of Economic Affairs

John Burton

JOHN BURTON was born in 1945, and educated at Worthing High School for Boys, the University College at Swansea, and the London School of Economics. From 1979 to 1983 he was a Lecturer in Industrial Economics in the Department of Industrial Economics and Business Studies, University of Birmingham, having previously lectured at Southampton University (1969-70) and Kingston Polytechnic (1971-79). In the summer of 1981 he was a visiting research fellow at the Heritage Foundation, Washington DC, and in 1981-82 he was a Nuffield Foundation social science research fellow. In Autumn to Spring 1985-86 he was on secondment as principal research officer for the Employment Research Centre, University of Buckingham.

He is the author of *Wage Inflation* (1972); *The Job-Support Machine* (1979); *The Future of American Trade Unions* (1982); (with J. T. Addison) *Trade Unions and Society* (1983); and of articles in numerous journals. For the IEA he has previously written 'Are Trade Unions a Public Good/'Bad'?: The Economics of the Closed Shop', in *Trade Unions: Public Goods or Public 'Bads'?* (IEA Readings No. 17, 1978); (with J. M. Buchanan and R. E. Wagner) *The Consequences of Mr Keynes* (Hobart Paper 78, 1978); 'Externalities, Property Rights, and Public Policy', in S. N. S. Cheung *et al.*, *The Myth of Social Cost* (Hobart Paper 82, 1978); 'Trade Unions' Role in the British Disease: An Interest in Inflation?', in *Is Monetarism Enough?* (IEA Readings No. 24, 1980); 'An Economic Commentary', in H. S. Ferns, *How Much Freedom for Universities?* (Occasional Paper 65, 1982); *Picking Losers . . .?* (Hobart Paper 99, 1983); *Why No Cuts?* (Hobart Paper 104, 1985); and articles in *Economic Affairs*.

John Burton joined the Institute of Economic Affairs as a Research Fellow in October 1983 and has been Research Director since 1984.

2

Fifty Years On: Background and Foreground

JOHN BURTON

BACKGROUND

The General Theory of Employment, Interest and Money by John Maynard Keynes was first published in England in February 1936.[1] It was an immediate success, and especially among many young academic economists on both sides of the Atlantic. Keynes himself had earlier written to George Bernard Shaw of his new work: '. . . I believe myself to be writing a book on economic theory which will largely revolutionise . . . the way the world thinks about economic problems'.[2]

Keynes had years earlier established a reputation as a brilliant and penetrating controversialist, most notably in his account and analysis of the Treaty of Versailles,[3] and also in his critique of Britain's return to the gold standard at the pre-war parity in 1925.[4] He had also established for himself a reputation as a serious, lucid and wide-ranging economist. His earlier works in technical economics over the quarter of a century preceding the publication of *The General Theory*, however, whilst often original and critical, were written within the mainstream of economic analysis at that time. Keynes was then mainly concerned in technical economics to refine the standard analysis of the link between money and the general level of prices—the quantity theory of money—and to spell out more clearly, as he saw it, the process by which it worked.[5]

The General Theory

The General Theory was a different kettle of fish. In this work Keynes challenged in a number of ways the foundations of

1 London: Macmillan.
2 Quoted in R. F. Harrod, *The Life of John Maynard Keynes*, London: Macmillan, 1951, p. 462.
3 J. M. Keynes, *The Economic Consequences of the Peace*, London: Macmillan, 1919.
4 J. M. Keynes, *The Economic Consequences of Mr. Churchill*, London: L. and V. Woolf, 1925.
5 J. M. Keynes, *A Treatise on Money*, New York: Harcourt, Brace, 1930.

the whole tradition of 'classical' economic doctrine,[6] including the teachings of his Cambridge mentors and colleagues, Alfred Marshall and (especially) A. C. Pigou.

In this book he redefined the main economic problem not as the allocation of scarce resources amongst competing ends—an idea embedded in a long tradition of economic thinking, and associated especially in Keynes's era with the late Professor Lionel Robbins[7]—but as the maintenance of aggregate demand and employment in the short run. New analytical economic concepts were advanced, such as the propensity to consume, liquidity preference, and effective demand.* Central emphasis in Keynes's 'introductory' Chapter II in *The General Theory* was put on the peculiarities of the labour market—or rather, quite specifically, on the nature of labour-supply decisions.[8] Other new themes, largely original to economics at that time, included the impact and pervasiveness of uncertainty in economic life,[9] and the consequent role of speculation in stock markets.

Moreover, in Keynes's analysis the stock of money in the economy was no longer seen as 'neutral' in its effects upon the economy, as it had been presented in at least some cruder renditions of the quantity theory. Keynes argued that changes in monetary conditions could influence 'real' variables such as the general levels of employment and output. 'Classical' (i.e., pre-Keynesian) economic analysis was therefore argued to be a 'special case' of the more general *General Theory*.

The General Theory was thus many things. It was a challenging onslaught against received economic theory, a cornucopia

---

[6] The term 'classical economics' was coined by Karl Marx, and was used by him to describe the line of thought developed by David Ricardo, James Mill, and their *predecessors*, such as Adam Smith. Keynes, however, used the term to cover also the 'neo-classical' *followers* of Ricardo, such as Marshall and Pigou.

[7] *An Essay on the Nature and Significance of Economic Science*, London: Macmillan, 1932 (2nd edn. 1935).

[8] J. T. Addison and J. Burton, 'Keynes' Analysis of Wages and Unemployment Revisited', *Manchester School*, March 1982, pp. 1-23.

[9] 'Decision-making under uncertainty, which Keynes had treated in his *A Treatise on Probability* [1921, reprinted in *The Collected Writings of John Maynard Keynes*, Vol. VIII, Macmillan/Cambridge University Press for The Royal Economic Society, 1973], is central to *The General Theory* . . .'. (H. P. Minsky, *John Maynard Keynes*, London: Macmillan, 1975, p. 66.)

*The Glossary (pp. 153-159) contains definitions of these and other terms.

of novel economic concepts, and the harbinger of a new politico-economic age in many Western countries: the so-called 'Age of Keynes'.

The Keynesian Revolution and the 'Age of Keynes'

The General Theory appeared as a new explanation of the events of the 1930s and specifically of the Great Contraction in the USA between 1929 and 1932. The preceding decade had generally been a period of growth and prosperity—except in the UK—but after 1929 unemployment increased dramatically across the world, accompanied by a severe fall in prices and business confidence. By 1932, the volume of industrial production in the USA was only just over half that in 1929, and the Dow-Jones average of stock prices had fallen from $125 (in 1929) to $27 (by 1932). In 1933, some 25 per cent of the civilian labour force of America was recorded as unemployed.[10]

Orthodox economic analysis at that time did not seem capable of explaining these dramatic events, whilst *The General Theory* seemed to do so. According to Keynes's new diagnosis, the transitional processes of a capitalist economy were not self-correcting, and there was no inbuilt tendency towards a stable equilibrium at full employment.

The precise implications for economic policy were not specified in *The General Theory*, but the general direction of Keynes's thinking was clear. If the macro-economy of the capitalist system was unstable, then government should step in to correct the imbalance via monetary, fiscal and investment policy.

In the post-war period this new view was to become the orthodoxy for UK economic policy. Although the precise dating of changes in policy and their acceptance by the majority of economists is difficult, there can be no doubt that the 'Keynesian Revolution' *did* occur. For the UK, the fundamental shift in the policy framework and outlook is usually ascribed to the White Paper on *Employment Policy*[11] of May 1944, which, nevertheless, did not commit post-war governments to target rates of unemployment, but talked only of the maintenance of 'high and stable'—rather than 'full'—employment.

[10]B. Mitchell, *Depression Decade*, New York: Reinhart, 1947.
[11]Cmd. 6527, HMSO, 1944.

By the 1950s advocates of Keynesian policy in all political parties were thoroughly wedded to 'fine-tuning' the economy by means of discretionary monetary and fiscal policy, so as to attain a low (say, 2 per cent) target rate of unemployment. The so-called 'Age of Keynes' had arrived. Since it is doubtful whether Keynes himself would have accepted that fine-tuning could achieve such unprecedentedly low rates of unemployment, it would be more accurate to say that the 'Age of Keynesianism' had arrived![12]

For a considerable period, Keynesian economic theory became the ruling paradigm in the teaching of economics in most institutions of higher education in the West, most notably in the UK. Indeed, in much teaching, micro-economics became relegated very much to a subordinate place—if it was not actually dropped altogether. Aggregative concepts along Keynesian lines, growth theory, and econometric models were now to become the fashionable areas of economic thought and analysis.

Government economic policy during the 1950s and 1960s in the UK, and certainly after 1964 in the USA, largely reflected these ideas. Central importance was placed upon macro-economic 'steering', to the neglect of the micro-foundations of economic development, such as the role of entrepreneurs, the discovery procedure of competitive markets, the evolution of financial mechanisms and instruments, the importance of a framework of stable law for investment and enterprise, and the effect of property rights upon economic endeavour and business efficiency.

The Emergence of 'Stagflation' and Doubts

At first, the Keynesian bias of policy did not appear to have harmful side-effects. The UK, for example, enjoyed low rates of recorded unemployment—sometimes below 1 per cent in the 1950s and averaging 2·4 per cent in the mid-1960s. Nor did the inflation cost of this macro 'full employment' at first seem high: over the whole period 1958-69, for example, the British rate of inflation averaged 3·8 per cent per year.

[12] T. W. Hutchison, *Keynes v. the 'Keynesians'* . . .?, London: Institute of Economic Affairs, Hobart Paperback No. 11, 1977.

In the 1970s the world-wide escalation of inflation combined with rising unemployment—a phenomenon known as 'stagflation'—to bring Keynesianism into doubt. Keynesian economic theory seemed unable to offer a robust explanation of stagflation, and Keynesian economists were driven to introduce *ad hoc* explanations such as union militancy, or vaguer 'socio-political' factors, or the power of Arab sheiks.[13] In sum, Keynesian economic policy, which by the 1960s had become based upon the notion of the Phillips curve,[14] seemed powerless to offer any solution to the problem of stagflation along orthodox Keynesian macro-manipulation lines; hence the Keynesian interest in and advocacy of wage and price controls.

These growing doubts about the applicability of Keynesianism were underpinned by a number of major developments in economic analysis in the 1960s and 1970s, which offered theoretical and empirical perspectives critical of Keynesianism from a variety of angles.

The Monetarist Re-interpretation

A major though not immediate impact was made by the publication in 1963 of *A Monetary History of the United States 1867-1960* by Milton Friedman and Anna J. Schwartz.[15] This *magnum opus* provided strong documentation for the view that the stock of money exerts a powerful effect on the level of nominal economic activity (i.e., money GDP), albeit with a long and variable lag. Interest centred specifically upon the authors' interpretation of the Great Contraction in the USA between 1929 and 1932. The standard Keynesian analysis of this event attributed the contraction to a collapse of investment—investment expenditure is the prime mover in the Keynesian system—against which monetary policy was im-

---

[13]J. T. Addison and J. Burton, 'The Sociopolitical Analysis of Inflation', *Weltwirtschaftliches Archiv*, Band 120, Heft 1, 1984, pp. 90-120.

[14]The Phillips curve presumes that there is a stable *negative* relationship between inflation and unemployment. Under stagflation, however, there is a positive relationship between them—unemployment and inflation rise together.

[15]Princeton: Princeton University Press for the National Bureau of Economic Research, 1963.

potent due to the existence of a liquidity trap.[16] On the contrary, Friedman and Schwartz argued that the Great Contraction provided savage testimony to the *power* of monetary policy. Mismanagement of the money supply by the Federal Reserve Board had caused a one-third *reduction* in the stock of money in the USA between 1929 and 1933, magnifying what might otherwise have been a mild recession into a major economic collapse.

This monetarist re-interpretation of history—of the 1930s experience—was followed by the development of the monetarist analysis of inflation, which was also applied (although not exclusively) to the post-war Keynesian period in advanced industrialised countries. In a highly influential presidential address to the American Economic Association, Milton Friedman re-introduced the role of price expectations to the analysis of inflation—a factor previously absent from Keynesian analyses based on Phillips curve lines—and presented his theory of the 'natural rate' of unemployment.[17] The central implication was that monetary policy could not be used to hold unemployment down permanently to some low target rate below its equilibrium (or 'natural') level, except at the cost of generating an *ever-accelerating* inflation. Thus the long-run viability of Keynesian policies, persistently pursued, was brought into question.[18] Instead, this new approach emphasised the alternative strategy of reducing the (natural) rate of unemployment by removing legislative barriers to, and microeconomic obstacles and frictions which prevented, higher employment.[19]

---

[16]That is, monetary policy was incapable of raising employment, because the demand for money had become infinitely elastic with respect to the nominal rate of interest, since all market participants assume that the latter cannot fall further, and must rise.

[17]M. Friedman, 'The Role of Monetary Policy', *American Economic Review*, Vol. 58, March 1968, pp. 1-17.

[18]Also, M. Friedman, *The Counter-Revolution in Monetary Theory*, London: IEA, Occasional Paper 33, 1970; M. Friedman, *Unemployment v. Inflation?*, London: IEA, Occasional Paper 44, 1975; M. Friedman, *Inflation and Unemployment: the New Dimension of Politics*, London: IEA, Occasional Paper 51, 1977.

[19]R. Miller and J. B. Wood, *What Price Unemployment?*, London: IEA, Hobart Paper 92, 1981.

The Resurgence of Austrian Economics

The monetarist critique of Keynesianism was complemented by a resurgence of interest in so-called Austrian economics.[20] Throughout the post-war heyday of Keynesianism, Professor Ludwig von Mises had remained a staunch and unbending critic from an Austrian perspective of what he saw as the fallacies of Keynesian reasoning and policy.[21] His scathing dismissal of Keynesianism as the promise to turn stones into bread had been generally ignored by an economics profession overwhelmingly wedded to Keynesian concepts and modelling techniques.[22] Friedrich Hayek, once Mises's pupil in Vienna, had clashed sharply with Keynes in the early 1930s over the appropriate framework for the analysis of monetary phenomena and fluctuations.[23] He subsequently re-directed his attention to what he then thought of as unrelated matters of methodology, political philosophy, and the nature of the process of co-ordination in a market economy. As a friend and colleague of Keynes, Hayek was aware of Keynes's capacity for changing his mind on both theory and policy, and had therefore regarded the 'general' theory as but 'a tract for the times', which Keynes might later recant. Thus a 'Keynesians vs. the Austrians' confrontation failed to emerge in the decades immediately following the Second World War.

Hayek's Nobel Prize for economic science in 1974, combined with a growing general appreciation of the profundity and breadth of his work, has led to more attention being paid to

[20]An introduction to, and overview of, Austrian economic thought is provided in S. C. Littlechild, *The Fallacy of the Mixed Economy*, London: IEA, Hobart Paper 80, 1978 (second edn., 1986).

[21]Mises had predicted the general nature of the inter-war depression as early as 1912, in the first, German, edition of his *Theory of Money and Credit*, which set out the Austrian analysis of the business cycle.

[22]L. von Mises, 'Stones into Bread: The Keynesian Miracle', in his *Planning for Freedom*, South Holland, Illinois: Libertarian Press, 1952, pp. 50-63.

[23]F. A. Hayek, 'Reflections on the Pure Theory of Money of Mr. Keynes', *Economica*, August 1931 and February 1932; J. M. Keynes, 'The Pure Theory of Money—A Reply to Dr. Hayek', and F. A. Hayek, 'A Rejoinder to Mr. Keynes', *Economica*, November 1931.

the Austrian critique of Keynesian theory and policy over the last decade.[24]

The essence of this critique is that Keynesianism, based on *macro*-economic or aggregative constructs, ignores the integrating role played by freely-formed market (relative) prices in co-ordinating diverse expectations throughout the economy. By thus ignoring the distortions and inflexibility of relative prices caused by union pressure, government edicts, and the 'wages floor' embedded in the labour market by the operation of the welfare state, Keynesians interpret the resulting unemployment to be solely the consequence of a deficiency of aggregate demand.[25]

Austrians also emphasise how monetary and fiscal policy changes—which in the Keynesian view have only *macro*-effects— cause disco-ordination in the *structure* of prices and production and thus create a maldistribution of resources.[26] To sustain this maldistribution, the rate of monetary expansion, and thus of inflation, must *continuously* be increased if symptoms of adjustment and depression are to be avoided. For Austrians, Keynesian policies of expansionism to deal with unemployment are like holding a tiger by the tail: it is extremely difficult to let go. The 'loosening' of the Medium-Term Financial Strategy in the UK since 1985 may turn out to be a telling instance of this grim judgement.

Expectations and the 'Fundamental Keynesian' View

The General Theory was much concerned with expectations; and, indeed, that work was characterised by the late Professor

[24]Many of Hayek's writings on this subject are collected in *A Tiger by the Tail: The Keynesian Legacy of Inflation*, London: IEA, Hobart Paperback 4, second edn., 1978. Also his *Full Employment at Any Price?*, London: IEA, Occasional Paper 45, 1975.

[25]Keynes himself in *The General Theory* did not deny the existence of both frictional and voluntary unemployment, but was more concerned to focus there upon 'involuntary' unemployment due to a deficiency of effective demand. His later writings just before World War II also reveal a strong appreciation of the frictional and structural sources of unemployment. Some Keynesian disciples after the war were, however, to neglect these matters almost totally in their single-minded advocacy of demand management to achieve low target rates of unemployment. (Cf. Hutchison, *op. cit.*)

[26]G. P. O'Driscoll, jr., and S. R. Shenoy, 'Inflation, Recession, Stagflation', in E. G. Dolan (ed.), *Foundations of Modern Austrian Economics*, Lawrence, Kansas: Sheed and Ward, 1976.

H. G. Johnson as a short-run model 'of an economy in which behaviour is governed by expectations about the future'.[27] However, Keynes provided within it no formal and general analysis of the formation of expectations. In Keynes's theoretical world, 'the basis of choice lies in vague, uncertain and shifting expectations, that have no firm foundation in circumstances'.[28]

It is on the basis of this inspiration from Keynes that the British economist G. L. S. Shackle has for long contested the rationale of Keynesian fine-tuning policies. If the real world is characterised by unexpected change, shifting expectations, and inconsistent plans, then '... how can any reliable [governmental] levers exist for managing it?'[29]

Shackle's doubts are challenging and in some ways complement the Austrian critique of Keynesianism based on the *fundamental* complexity of economic life, in comparison with the 'hydraulic' Keynesian vision of the economy as a small set of stable relationships between macro-variables (such as total consumer spending and aggregate disposable income). Yet Shackle's line of analysis—which has been labelled as the 'fundamental Keynesian' position, in contrast to the 'hydraulic Keynesian' school that dominated post-war thought—has found few takers in contemporary economics. One reason may be that if all of economic life is but a 'skein of subtle influences', of uncertainty and shifting expectations, so that, as the fundamental Keynesian view asserts, rational economic decision-making is logically impossible, how can economists analyse it?

There is much of subtlety in Shackle's work on uncertainty and expectations in economic life which has perhaps been insufficiently attended to by a post-war economics profession more taken up with computing and data bases. This is precisely why the 'fundamental Keynesian' perspective seemed bound to lack followers. Econometric testing of hypotheses requires *some* clear assumptions about relationships, *including*

[27]H. G. Johnson, 'The General Theory After Twenty-Five Years', *American Economic Review*, Vol. LI, No. 2, May 1961, pp. 1-17.

[28]A. Coddington, 'Keynesian Economics: The Search for First Principles', *Journal of Economic Literature*, Vol. 14, No. 4, December 1976, pp. 1,258-73.

[29]G. L. S. Shackle, *Epistemics and Economics*, Cambridge: Cambridge University Press, 1972.

the formation of expectations (even if shifting). The success of the rational expectations revolution has been in filling this gap whilst the 'fundamental Keynesian' perspective has not 'taken off'.[30]

The Rational Expectations Revolution

The monetarist analysis of inflation and unemployment initiated by Friedman, as well as the 'new micro-economics' of inflation and unemployment developed by Professor E. S. Phelps and others,[31] both pointed to an incongruence between the Age of Keynesianism and a postulate of *The General Theory*. Keynes had assumed that workers would accept *real* wage cuts, if effected by an increase in the price level with stable money wages, whereas they would not accept money wage cuts to bring about an equivalent fall in real wages. The Phillips curve hypothesis was essentially a dynamic version of this idea—that workers suffered from 'money illusion', being interested in the level (or rate of growth) of their *money* wages, and not in their real spending power.

Phelps and Friedman had warned that strong and persistent inflationary tendencies would eventually erode money illusion. It would not be possible to fool all of the workers all of the time. In the inflationary environment of the Age of Keynesianism, workers and firms would form expectations of future inflation and seek to bargain over *real* wages.

Expectations, specifically about higher prices, could no longer be ignored in either macro-economic or micro-economic analysis. The initial reaction of economists was to augment the Phillips curve idea by 'allowing for' expectations, assuming that *past* movements of the price level were 'extrapolated' to form 'adaptive' expectations.[32] But the models built around

---

[30]It is interesting to note that both Professor (now Emeritus) Shackle, the most noted fundamental Keynesian of our times, and the current British leader of the rational expectations school, Professor Patrick Minford, rose to pre-eminence intellectually at the University of Liverpool. Clearly there is something in the air at Liverpool which encourages economic thought on expectations. . .

[31]E. S. Phelps *et al.*, *Micro-economic Foundations of Employment and Inflation Theory*, New York: Norton, 1970.

[32]That is, expectations of inflation were assumed to be a weighted average of past levels, with the weights declining as more distant episodes/periods were considered.

this idea failed the test of prediction in the 1970s, with its experience of persistent stagflation (described earlier).[33] This is where the idea of rational expectations came in. The idea had been introduced by Professor J. F. Muth much earlier,[34] but was not applied to the issue of Keynesian economic policy until the work of Professor Robert E. Lucas, jr., in the early 1970s.[35] Unlike the vague and shifting patterns of expectations assumed in the fundamental Keynesian view, Muth and Lucas assumed that most dynamic modelling of the time simply did not assume *enough* rationality about the formation of expectations. Indeed, they assumed that expectations about future events are essentially the same as the relevant predictions of economic theory. This does not mean that all decision-makers are economic theoreticians, but rather that the known empirical regularities of business and economic life which are the subject matter of economic theorising also serve as the basis for economic decision-making. It certainly does not mean that either economic theoreticians or business decision-makers are omniscient, or that we live in a world of perfect competition with perfect and free information.

This is not the place to review the extensive literature on the rational expectations hypothesis, which has manifold implications for the whole of economic and econometric theory. What is, however, important for present purposes is that the rational expectations approach undermined the possibility of fine-tuning on orthodox Keynesian lines. The new theory indicated that if government were to act on a consistent pattern of macro-economic intervention—whether with stabilising or de-stabilising intentions—this pattern of behaviour would be discovered, and taken into account by other decision-

[33]C. F. Christ, 'Judging the Performance of Econometric Models of the U.S. Economy', *International Economic Review*, Vol. 16, No. 1, February 1975, pp. 54-74.

[34]J. F. Muth, 'Rational Expectations and the Theory of Price Movements', *Econometrica*, Vol. 29, No. 3, July 1961, pp. 315-35. Also his 'Optimal Properties of Exponentially Weighted Forecasts', *Journal of the American Statistical Association*, Vol. 55, No. 209, June 1960, pp. 299-306.

[35]Lucas's highly influential series of papers are collected in his *Studies in Business Cycle Theory*, Oxford: Basil Blackwell, 1981. A useful survey of the rational expectations literature, which traces its connections with Austrian economic thought, is provided by B. Kantor, 'Rational Expectations and Economic Thought', *Journal of Economic Literature*, Vol. XVII, December 1979, pp. 1,422-41.

makers. Regular policy actions, in other words, would affect the response of the economy, so that the behaviour of the economy *cannot* be 'policy invariant', as much naïve Keynesian modelling of the post-war period assumed.[36] This effect has been conceded even by those remaining advocates of Keynesian stabilisation policy who still see some role for it, under certain conditions.[37]

It was once fashionable to dismiss the idea of rational expectations formation, but there is now quiet acceptance in the world of economics that it is no mere piece of sophisticated, armchair theorising. Unlike the expectations views of fundamental Keynesianism, this hypothesis has proved useful in understanding both empirical regularities and contemporary events.[38]

Public Choice and the Motives of Government

The development and success of the rational expectations hypothesis has undermined the Keynesian supposition that government can manipulate the economy like a puppet on a string because the 'puppet' will try to take into account the string-pullings of the manipulator. Behind this analysis lies the further question of the motives of the string-puller. Government is a major actor on the economic scene in all modern countries and intervenes from complex motives. What, then, is it trying to do when 'manipulating' the economy, along Keynesian (or other) lines? These and related questions have been raised by the developing public-choice school of economics, based primarily in the United States.

An underlying supposition of all of John Maynard Keynes's

---

[36]E. C. Prescott, 'Should Control Theory Be Used for Economic Stabilisation?', in K. Brunner and A. H. Meltzer (eds.), 'Optimal Policies, Control Theory and Technology Exports', *Journal of Monetary Economics*, Supplement, Vol. 7, 1977, pp. 13-38.

[37]For example, S. Fischer, 'Long-Term Contracts, Rational Expectations and the Optimal Money Supply Rule', *Journal of Political Economy*, Vol. 85, No. 1, February 1977, pp. 191-205, and E. S. Phelps and J. B. Taylor, 'Stabilising Powers of Monetary Policy under Rational Expectations', *Journal of Political Economy*, Vol. 85, No. 1, February 1977, pp. 163-90.

[38]P. Minford, 'From Macro to Micro via Rational Expectations', in M. Anderson (ed.), *The Unfinished Agenda*, London: IEA, 1986, pp. 105-14.

work on economic policy has been summarised by his biographer, the late Sir Roy Harrod, in the phrase 'the presuppositions of Harvey Road':

'We have seen that he [Keynes] was strongly imbued with what I have called the presuppositions of Harvey Road. One of these presuppositions may perhaps be summarised in the idea that the government of Britain was and would continue to be in the hands of an intellectual aristocracy using the method of persuasion'.[39]

No. 6, Harvey Road was the Keynes family home: John Maynard was the son of a Cambridge don and that city's first lady mayor. It provided a Victorian and Edwardian environment of academic values, of devotion to the 'public interest', and of a confident presumption that the interpretation and implementation of policy would remain in the hands of an intellectual aristocracy of which the Keynes family was a notable example. Keynes did not envisage the application of his policy views in a vulgar contemporary political setting, in which parties of all persuasions are continuously tempted to yield to such pressures as numerous private vested-interest groups, including the bureaucracy, and the necessity of vote-garnering in order to win elections.

It was upon this political naïveté of the Keynesian theory of economic policy in contemporary democracy that Professors J. M. Buchanan and R. E. Wagner were to fasten in their public-choice study of Keynesianism.[40] As developed by disciples of Keynes, Keynesianism calls for fine-tuning of the economy, by means of counter-cyclical macro-economic engineering. Essentially it says that government should not balance its own budget but, rather, should deliberately de-stabilise it in the interests of attaining full employment without inflation.

The Buchanan-Wagner analysis points out that politicians have unequal incentives as between running budget deficits and surpluses. A budget surplus imposes immediate political costs, whilst a deficit always yields immediate political gains—

[39]R. F. Harrod, *op. cit.*, pp. 192-93.

[40]J. M. Buchanan and R. E. Wagner, *Democracy in Deficit: The Political Legacy of Lord Keynes*, New York: Academic Press, 1977. For a British application of the analysis, J. M. Buchanan, J. Burton and R. E. Wagner, *The Consequences of Mr Keynes*, London: IEA, Hobart Paper 78, 1978.

with the economic costs following later. Without a constitutional requirement to balance the budget, the tendency will
be for governments to prefer deficits to surpluses. The
Keynesian Revolution, in short, 'let the politicians loose' to
indulge in political self-interest.

The evidence for such a bias in political choice under a
Keynesian fiscal constitution is clear, in Britain, the USA,
France, West Germany—and spectacularly so in Italy where
the deficit currently mounts to around 15 per cent of GDP.[41]

FOREGROUND

The Demise of Keynesianism?

So much for the general background of economic events and
developments, which half a century after the publication of
The General Theory had led to some disillusion with Keynesianism
in both the groves of academe and the corridors of power.

The most striking example of this change was perhaps the
explicit adoption of monetary targets in the land of Keynes's
birth from the mid-1970s, later formalised as the Medium-Term
Financial Strategy (MTFS), introduced in 1980. Yet this
general development has by no means been confined to the
UK. Confidence in Keynesian demand management as a cure-
all for economic ills has certainly declined throughout Western
countries and beyond. The abandonment of an overtly
Keynesian policy to reduce unemployment by the socialist
government of President Mitterrand in France in 1982, after
only two years of its operation, underlines the new political
inhibition about all-out Keynesianism.

Can we therefore say that Keynesianism is now 'dead'? For
a number of reasons the answer must be 'No'. First, many
eminent and reputable economists—including Professors
Lawrence Klein and James Tobin in the USA; Professors
James Meade and Frank Hahn in the UK—retain elements of

---

[41]A. Martino, 'Italian Lessons on the Welfare State', *Economic Affairs*, Vol. 6, No.
5, June/July 1986, pp. 18-25.

Keynesianism in their thought and advocacy of policy. Indeed, it may well be that a majority of practising economists still adheres to Keynesianism, though most in modified form.[42] Second, concern about high and persistent unemployment in the 1980s continues to fuel the desire for a return to the 'golden age' of Keynesianism. It is not only union and church leaders but politicians of all parties who still call for 'reflation' without understanding the inflationary and other problems involved in such a simplistic strategy. Meanwhile, more cautious economists, who do acknowledge these risks and difficulties, have sought to devise programmes that will, they hope, minimise the inflation cost by targetting expenditure upon labour-intensive projects for the unskilled.[43] Thus the debate on Keynesian economic policies remains very much on the agenda.

A third reason for suspecting that Keynesianism as a policy alternative is unlikely to wither away, whatever the intellectual environment, arises from the public-choice analysis of budgetary financing referred to above. In the absence of a binding constitutional rule constraining government to balance its own budget, the stark implication of that analysis is that the temptation for politicians to run perpetual deficits will persist. It follows that policies such as the MTFS, which envisaged a generally declining budget deficit over a number of years, may not prove sufficient to prevent political opportunism. We might take heed of the Reagan plan of 1980 to balance the Federal budget by 1984. The present deficit of over $150 billion a year demonstrates that politics eventually triumphed over the declared goal of fiscal prudence.[44]

A fourth reason why interest in *The General Theory*, and its implications, is unlikely to die concerns the nature of both the author and the book. Interest in Keynes is unlikely to flag

[42]In 1981 some 364 British academic economists signed a petition critical of Mrs Thatcher's monetary and fiscal strategies, from a vaguely Keynesian perspective. It is doubtful that a similar number could have been found to sign a counter-petition.

[43]Charter for Jobs, *We Can Cut Unemployment*, London, 1985; R. Layard, 'On Tackling Unemployment', *Economic Affairs*, Vol. 5, No. 4, July-September, 1985, pp. 47-48.

[44]D. A. Stockman, *The Triumph of Politics*, London: Bodley Head, 1986.

because of his stature, of which Professor Milton Friedman has written:

> 'Had the *General Theory* never been written, Keynes would never-theless have deservedly been regarded as one of the great econ-omists of all time—to be listed in the pantheon of great British economists along with Adam Smith, David Ricardo, John Stuart Mill, William Stanley Jevons, and Alfred Marshall'.[45]

Moreover, the very nature of *The General Theory*, both as literature and as economic analysis, continues to invite specu-lation about its meaning. Even committed Keynesians openly admit that it 'contains confusions and conflicts'.[46] As Professor Robert M. Solow has remarked:

> '. . . there are several strands in the *General Theory*, and Keynes need not have been conscious that they are only partially con-sistent, or even not consistent all'.[47]

Whether or not this is true, the opaque character of *The General Theory* has over the years provoked a large number of differing interpretations of its meaning, theoretical structure, and im-plications. Even if Keynesianism as economic policy were to be abandoned everywhere, interest among economists in these questions, and in the place of *The General Theory* in the history of economic thought, would persist.

Fifty Years On

Thus, fifty years on, controversies continue to surround *The General Theory*. Neither the work of Keynes, nor the policy of Keynesianism, is dead and buried. Many important questions remain concerning *The General Theory* and its implications. It was to examine some of them that the Institute of Economic Affairs invited 10 distinguished economists from America and Britain to contribute essays to this volume.

[45]M. Friedman, 'The Keynes Centenary: A Monetarist Reflects', *Economist*, 4 June 1983.

[46]G. Routh, *The Origin of Economic Ideas*, London: Macmillan, 1975, p. 273.

[47]R. M. Solow, 'Alternative Approaches to Macro-economic Theory: A Partial View', *Canadian Journal of Economics*, Vol. 12, No. 3, pp. 339-54.

Among the many controversies over the meaning and content of *The General Theory*, one particularly influential interpretation has been developed by Professors A. Leijonhufvud[48] and R. W. Clower,[49] which asserts that underlying Keynes's macro-economics is a sophisticated micro-economic analysis of disequilibrium processes in a monetary economy. To examine this contention, and more generally to assess the place of *The General Theory* in the history of economic thought, we asked Professor L. Yeager to write on the intellectual legacy of Keynes. Professor Yeager is known as an authority on the textual content and theoretical structure of *The General Theory*, and his new essay should bring his analysis to the attention of a much wider body of students and interested laymen who do not feel at home in the arcane world of economic journals.

The author of the following essay, Dr Milton Friedman, will hardly require an introduction to any reader. The substance of his position in the 'monetarist *vs.* the Keynesians' debate continues to excite academic controversy, and is widely discussed in the media (although not always accurately). We invited Professor Friedman to concentrate less on the theoretical side of *The General Theory*, and more on its political legacy and relevance for the contemporary school of public choice.

Like the two previous authors, Professor Karl Brunner is also an eminent monetary theorist. He has also written extensively on methodological issues in economics and the social sciences more generally. His essay here concentrates on the methodology of *The General Theory*, and relates this both to its economics and to Keynes's view on policy matters. As with Friedman, he is congenial to Keynes's methodological approach, but he is unsympathetic to Keynes's, and the Keynesians', influence upon public policy. He makes the important point that classical liberalism and Keynesianism are two different types of 'product', as viewed from the perspective of their saleability in the political market, and that the choice

---

[48] *On Keynesian Economics and the Economics of Keynes*, Oxford: Oxford University Press, 1968; and his *Keynes and the Classics*, London: IEA, Occasional Paper 30, 1969.

[49] 'The Keynesian Counter-Revolution: A Theoretical Appraisal', in F. H. Hahn and F. Brechling (eds.), *The Theory of Interest Rates*, London: Macmillan, 1965, pp. 103-25.

between them in this market—by coalitions, interest groups, bureaucrats and governments—may not reflect their relative intellectual strengths.

The foregoing essays all deal with ideas and their impacts upon policy and the economy. The next paper, by Professor M. R. Darby and Dr J. R. Lothian, is primarily concerned with influences running in the other direction—from economic events to the world of ideas, and consequently their perceptions, status, and acceptance or otherwise. Specifically they concentrate upon the nature and impact of macro-economic events in the two decades which have been important in determining the standing of Keynesian ideas: the 1930s and the 1970s. Drawing upon evidence from both the USA and the UK, they find that Keynes misconstrued the nature of the admittedly unusual events in the 1930s in his *General Theory*, because of his failure to distinguish between nominal and real rates of interest;[50] and thus that '*The General Theory* was written to explain perceived empirical paradoxes [of the times] that did not exist'. The illusory explanatory power of *The General Theory*, however, led to the post-war adoption of Keynesian policies— with inflationary consequences that became increasingly world-wide, especially in the early 1970s due to the rising trend of American monetary growth combined with fixed exchange rates.

The Darby-Lothian paper thus neatly attributes the 'discrediting' of the Keynesian ideas that they diagnose (not only aggregate demand-management but also the Bretton Woods system[51]) to their very adoption. This, however, raises Professor Brunner's point yet again. The political fate of economic policies is not necessarily determined by economic research into their empirical validity (or at least not by that alone).

Subsequent essays in the volume all deal with specific topics raised by *The General Theory*, which are of vital contemporary concern, fifty years later.

[50]That is, the nominal rate adjusted to account for the rate of inflation or deflation of the general level of prices anticipated by borrowers and lenders.

[51]The 'Bretton Woods system' of fixed exchange rates was established at a major international conference (attended by 44 countries) in Bretton Woods, New Hampshire, in 1944 (although not set in motion until 1945). Keynes played a leading part in the undertaking and outcome of the conference.

The Behaviour of Consumption and Savings

The central concept of *The General Theory* is generally thought to be the consumption function, which basically determines the magnitude of the multiplier in Keynesian theory.[52] The multiplier in turn is crucial to the efficacy of Keynesian demand management strategies, because the 'fiscal policy multiplier' determines their eventual impact on national income and employment.

It is the lessons taught by 50 years of experience and research of such issues that Professor Sir Alan Walters examines in his contribution. His conclusions will doubtless attract attention not only because of his stature as an applied econometrician and wide-ranging economist, but also because of his role as a personal economic adviser to the Prime Minister after 1981.

His analysis starts from the finding that the behaviour of aggregate consumption and savings has become far less predictable in the 1970s and 1980s than formerly; moreover, it seems to be virtually inexplicable when international differences are considered—not only from a Keynesian but also from a Friedmanian perspective. It appears that during this period real fiscal policy multipliers have not only become lower, but may now even be 'perverse and negative'. Yet, most interestingly, Sir Alan finds the answers to these economic perplexities of our times within *The General Theory* itself, in a revised form of Keynes's analysis (Ch. 12) of the 'state of confidence' held by businesses, investors, and the market. Specifically, he argues that confidence is very much affected by the *credibility* of government policy, and he therefore expects that the new policy environment established since 1981 in the UK will cause the economic record of the 1980s to be strikingly different from that of the earlier post-war decades.

---

[52]The multiplier is the ultimate increase in real national income resulting from an increase in so-called 'autonomous' expenditure, such as government spending. The notion of an (employment) multiplier was first propounded by Keynes's Cambridge colleague, R. F. (now Lord) Kahn, some years before *The General Theory*, in his 'The Relation of Home Investment to Unemployment', *Economic Journal*, June 1931.

Rational Expectations and Voters' Behaviour

The theme of expectations is taken up in the next essay, by Professor Patrick Minford, the acknowledged British leader of the rational expectations school of economic thought and modelling. He contrasts his view of the formation of expectations with the Keynesian hypothesis and exposes its implications for economic policy, specifically as for policies of gradual deceleration, advocated by many monetarists, and policies of reflation via larger budget deficits, advocated by many Keynesians.

The Minford analysis departs from other assessments in this collection in two important ways. First, whilst both Minford's and Walters's views are at one on the importance of the credibility of government policy in determining the 'expectational climate', Walters would be closer to Keynes than Minford in accepting the need to take account of 'the subtleties of market sentiment and psychology', which may elude the econometric modeller. Second, although Professor Minford is as strong an advocate of balanced budgets as Friedman, he is apparently more sanguine than either the latter or Professor Brunner about the possibility of achieving such a policy goal *without* the constitutional disciplining of government. Minford, in contrast with Brunner, argues that rational voters will choose non-Keynesian policy-makers and governments in preference to Keynesians.

The differences here would seem to stem from underlying assumptions about the nature of choice in the political market. Minford's view is that rational voters will employ rational expectations in making the political choice between alternative governments. The implicit view of Friedman and Brunner, and explicitly of Buchanan and Wagner,[53] is that, although voters are largely self-interested, the complicated and public goods character[54] of political choice (compared with market choice) may lead voters to make 'rationally ignorant' decisions.

[53]*Op cit.*

[54]Political choice has the characteristic of a 'public good' because the fully-informed individual making such a choice collects only a minute part of the resulting social benefits of informed choice. Consequently, it is irrational to be politically well-informed. The theory of rational voter ignorance was first advanced in A. Downs, *An Economic Theory of Democracy*, Harper and Row, New York, 1957.

Elements of economic insight exist in both views; history will eventually reveal which was the more correct.

Secular Stagnation, International Trade and Unemployment

The *General Theory* was primarily concerned with the workings of the macro-economy in the short run, and also with an isolated, 'closed' economy, ignoring flows of trade and international money. Many—particularly Alvin Hansen, Keynes's chief American disciple of the 1930s and 1940s—also read into *The General Theory* the hypothesis that the capitalist economy was doomed to long-run, secular stagnation.[55] Moreover, *The General Theory* did have things to say about trade policy and international monetary relations which are related both to the secular stagnation thesis and to Keynes's later proposals on the international economic order (elaborated at the Bretton Woods conference).

It is these aspects of Keynes's work and thought that Professor Michael Beenstock examines here. He finds that Keynes was indeed a secular stagnation theorist, but that there is no empirical evidence for this view. He also rejects Keynes's views on the stabilisation of international commodity prices and the management of exchange rates. Instead, he calls for the liberalisation of labour and product markets so that wages and prices become more flexible.

This matter leads on directly to the final essay of the volume, by Professor Alan Budd, which deals with the relevance of Keynes's analysis to unemployment, both then and now. Many would see contemporary unemployment as the most serious problem of the times and perhaps recall that 1986 marks the 50th anniversary not only of *The General Theory* but also of the Jarrow march against unemployment.

After a brief review of theories and categories of unemployment, Professor Budd examines the relevance of Keynes's views to the employment situation and to present policy. He concludes, tantalisingly, that Keynes's challenge to orthodox

[55]A. Hansen, 'Mr. Keynes on Underemployment Equilibrium', *Journal of Political Economy*, Vol. XLIV, No. 5, October 1936; and 'Some Notes on Terborgh's "The Bogey of Economic Maturity",' *Review of Economics and Statistics*, Vol. XXVIII, No. 1, February 1946.

thinking on unemployment remains valid today, but that we cannot 'simply apply Keynesian solutions to today's problems'. He also finds that the current Thatcher Government's policies towards unemployment have a more mixed intellectual pedigree than is commonly assumed.

The constitution of the Institute requires it formally to dissociate its Trustees, Directors and Advisers from the analysis of its authors, but it offers these stimulating essays by distinguished economic scholars as a contribution to a debate that continues to divide economists half a century after the appearance of *The General Theory*.[56] It is no small tribute to John Maynard Keynes that this should be so.

---

[56]A wider evaluation of Keynes's thinking, writings and activities covering the whole span of his life and career is to be released worldwide by the IEA as a Hobart Video in 1987.

1. The Keynesian Heritage in Economics

LELAND B. YEAGER

Ludwig von Mises Distinguished Professor of Economics,
Auburn University, Alabama

Leland B. Yeager

LELAND B. YEAGER graduated from Oberlin College with a B.A. degree in 1948, before taking his M.A. and Ph.D. at Columbia University in 1949 and 1952. He taught at Texas A & M College in 1949-50, at the University of Maryland from 1952 to 1957, and at the University of Virginia from 1957 to 1984, holding the Paul Goodloe McIntire Chair from 1969 on. Since 1985 he has been the Ludwig von Mises Distinguished Professor of Economics at Auburn University, Alabama. He has held visiting professorships at Southern Methodist University, the University of California at Los Angeles, New York University, and George Mason University, Fairfax, Virginia.

Professor Yeager has written many books and articles on monetary theory, international economics, and political economy, including *International Monetary Relations* (1966), (jointly with David Tuerck) *Foreign Trade and US Policy* (1976), and (with collaborators) *Experiences with Stopping Inflation* (1981).

26

The Keynesian Heritage in Economics
LELAND B. YEAGER

Keynes the Salesman

What difference has the *General Theory* made? How do economics and economic policy differ from what they would have been if Keynes had never lived?

Keynes sold the economics profession on concern with the macro problems of employment and demand. This concern was not new. Even—or especially—among Chicago economists in the early years of the Great Depression, it had already led to policy recommendations sounding remarkably Keynesian [Davis, 1971]. But understanding was far from general, as one can verify by browsing through Joseph Dorfman's *Economic Mind in American Civilisation* [1959] and by considering how experimental and eclectic anti-depression policy was. Keynes saw and provided what would gain attention—harsh polemics, sardonic passages, bits of esoteric and shocking doctrine. It helps a doctrine make a splash, as Harry Johnson [1971] suggested, to possess the right degree of difficulty—not so much as to discourage those who would thrill at being revolutionaries, yet enough to allow those who think they understand it to regard themselves as an élite vanguard.

If anyone should argue that pro-spending policies inspired by Keynesian doctrines contributed to general prosperity in the industrialised countries for roughly two decades after World War II, I would concede the point. It took roughly that long for expectations to become attuned to what was happening, for the Phillips unemployment/inflation trade-off to break down, and for expansionary policies to waste their impact in price inflation rather than maintain the desired real stimulus. The longer-run effects of Keynesianism are another story.

What Keynes 'Crowded Out'

Even in its early years, Keynesianism may have been a misfortune. Sounder developments in economic theory might have

27

gained influence had not Keynesianism crowded them off the intellectual scene. What Clark Warburton has called 'monetary disequilibrium theory' already had an honourable tradition, extending back at least as far as David Hume in 1752 and P. N. Christiernin in 1761.[1] Even earlier in that century, a rudimentary version evidently found successful expression in policy in several American colonies [Lester 1939/1970, Chs. III, IV, V]. Warburton's own efforts to extend the theory and the statistical evidence for it in the 1940s and 1950s were robbed of attention by the then-prevalent Keynesianism.

A sound approach to macro-economics, in my view, runs as follows (it largely overlaps what W. H. Hutt teaches in his own idiosyncratic terminology). Fundamentally, behind the veil of money, people specialise in producing particular goods and services to exchange them for the specialised outputs of other people. Any particular output thus constitutes demand for other (non-competing) outputs. Since supply constitutes demand in that sense, there can be no fundamental problem of deficiency of aggregate demand. Even in a depression, men and women are willing to work, produce, exchange, and consume. In particular, employers are willing to hire more workers and produce more goods if only they could find customers, while unemployed workers are willing and eager to become customers if only they could be back at work earning money to spend.

This doctrine is not just a crude, Panglossian version of Say's Law. It goes on to recognise that something may be obstructing the transactions whereby people might gratify unsatisfied desires to the benefit of all concerned. It inquires into what the obstruction might be. In Hutt's version, villains are obstructing the market forces that would otherwise move wages and prices to market-clearing levels.

Clark Warburton offered a different emphasis. As he argued [e.g., 1966, selection 1, esp. pp. 26-27], a tendency towards equilibrium rather than disequilibrium is inherent in the logic of a market economy. Whenever, therefore, markets are quite generally and conspicuously failing to clear, some essentially exogenous disturbance must have occurred, a disturbance

---

[1] Pehr Niclas Christiernin (1725-1799) was a Swedish philosopher and economist at the University of Uppsala.

pervasive enough to resist quick, automatic correction. In a depression, what bars people from accomplishing all the exchanges of each other's goods and services that they desire is a deficient real quantity of money. Such a deficiency could arise either from shrinkage of the money supply or from its failure to keep pace with the demand for money associated with real economic growth. Even then, the real money supply could remain adequate if people marked down their prices and wages sufficiently and promptly. Price and wage 'stickiness' is, however, sensible from the standpoint of individual decision-makers, even though that stickiness, in the face of monetary disturbances, has painful macro-economic consequences. (An adaptation of this account, drawing on an analogy between levels and trends of prices, can handle the case of 'stagflation'. It is unnecessary to assume, as simplistic Keynesian analysis does, that inflation and depression are exact opposites associated respectively with too much and too little aggregate demand.)

Re-interpretations of Keynes

Robert Clower [1965] and Axel Leijonhufvud [1968], and other writers in their tradition, have interpreted Keynes as espousing a good part of the theory just sketched out. (They ignored its earlier expositors.) They emphasise such concepts as the absence of the Walrasian auctioneer, incomplete and costly and imperfect information, false price signals, sluggish or poorly co-ordinated price adjustments, quantity adjustments besides price adjustments, the dual-decision process (i.e., people's decisions about trying to buy or sell in some markets depend on whether or not they succeed in carrying out desired transactions in other markets), and the 'income-constrained process' (the infectiousness of failure or success in accomplishing transactions). In brief, information gaps and other frictions bar the swift, co-ordinated, and appropriate re-adjustment of interdependent yet separately decided prices. In the face of pervasive disturbances, notably monetary disturbances, the price system cannot maintain or readily restore equilibrium.

Clower and Leijonhufvud admit that Keynes did not explicitly state what they suppose he meant. They offer excuses for him. In trying to break free from orthodoxy, he was handicapped by unavailability of the required concepts. The orthodox doctrine he was attacking had not yet been spelled out explicitly enough. Still, ample excuses for not having done or said something are not, after all, the same as actually having done or said it.

Was Keynes a 'Keynesian'?

Despite Clower and Leijonhufvud, much of what Keynes says in the *General Theory* does indeed resemble the supposedly vulgar Keynesianism of the textbooks. If Keynes really was a disequilibrium theorist, why did he make so much of the possibility of *equilibrium* at underemployment? Why did he minimise and almost deny the automatic forces conceivably working, however sluggishly, towards full-employment equilibrium? Why did he repeatedly worry (as in the *General Theory*, p. 347) about 'a chronic tendency throughout human history for the propensity to save to be stronger than the inducement to invest'? 'The desire of the individual to augment his personal wealth by abstaining from consumption', Keynes continued (p. 348), 'has usually been stronger than the inducement to the entrepreneur to augment the national wealth by employing labour on the construction of durable assets'. Why did he say (p. 31) that a rich community would find it harder than a poor community to fill its saving gap with investment? Why did he argue (p. 105) that the more fully investment has already provided for the future, the less scope remains for making still further provision? Keynes's hints at the stagnation thesis and in favour of government responsibility for total investment also suggest that he worried about *real* factors making for a chronic tendency for demand to prove deficient. So does his emphasis on a 'fundamental psychological law' of consumption spending and his hints in favour of income redistribution (p. 373) to raise the overall propensity to consume.

His worries about excessive thrift date back to before the *General Theory*. Recall, for example, his parable in the *Treatise on Money* [1930, I, pp. 176-78] about the devastation wrought by a thrift campaign in an economy of banana plantations; he goes on to compare his own theory with the over-saving or under-consumption theories of Mentor Bouniatian, J. A.

Hobson, W. T. Foster and W. Catchings. Keynes's banana parable describes too simple an economy to be amenable to interpretation along the lines of Clower and Leijonhufvud. The parable does not even mention money. Clearly Keynes was worrying about over-saving as such.

Keynes's emphasis in the *General Theory* on a definite multiplier relation between changes in investment and in total income also suggests concern about difficulties more deep-seated than the Clower-Leijonhufvud analysis describes. This analysis interprets Keynes in terms of the dynamics of income-constrained processes* associated with deficiencies of information, inadequately adjusted prices, and the attendant disco-ordination. It seems significant that W. H. Hutt, whose theory of cumulative deterioration in a depression is remarkably similar to that of Clower and Leijonhufvud [Glazier, 1970], believes he is expounding a doctrine quite different from what he considers to be the crudities of Keynes.

George Brockway [1986, p. 13] provides an extreme example of crude, popularised Keynesianism. Possibly Keynes's greatest contribution

> 'was his demonstration that in a capitalist system (or in any system that is advanced much beyond bare subsistence), glut is not only possible; it is always imminent'.

Liquidity preference makes the economy unable 'to buy and pay for everything it produces; hence a glut'. Brockway finds 'disgusting and stupid' the attempt being made in the United States nowadays 'to "balance" the budget and thus reduce government expenditures at the very moment they should be expanded'.

'Was Keynes a "Keynesian"?' Contradicting Leijonhufvud's thesis, Herschel Grossman in effect answers 'Yes'—and properly, in my view [Yeager, 1973]: '. . . Keynes' thinking was both substantially in accord with that of his populisers and similarly deficient' [Grossman, 1972, p. 26]. He provided no adequate micro-economic foundation for his macro-theory. His treatment of the demand for labour, in particular, is inconsistent with the Clower-Leijonhufvud interpretation. In-

* Glossary, p. 155.

stead of focussing on the labour-market consequences of disequilibrium in the market for current output, Keynes accepted the classical view that unemployment in a depression derives from an excessive real wage-rate. Keynes had in mind nothing like Clower's interpretation of the consumption function and simply offered an *ad hoc* formulation instead. Neither Keynes's writings nor the ensuing controversy and popularisation accomplished a shift away from a classical analytical with such writers as Patinkin and Clower.

Professor Allan Meltzer is another economist who does not accept the Clower-Leijonhufvud interpretation of the *General Theory* as emphasising the supposedly contagious failure of markets to clear because of sticky or malco-ordinated prices [Meltzer 1981, esp. pp. 49, 59; also Meltzer 1983]. Keynes was indeed concerned whether investment would be adequate to fill the savings gap at full employment. Investment tended to be inadequate—not always, but on the average over time—because investors' long-term expectations were bedevilled by uncertainty (non-quantifiable contingencies, not mere risks that might be estimated). Because expectations were poorly rooted in objective, measurable circumstances, changes in investors' 'animal spirits' tended to be contagious. Because investment thus fluctuated around a sub-optimal level, so did total output and employment. Some sort of government planning of large segments of investment seemed advisable as a remedy.

For Keynes, as also interpreted by Meltzer, then, macroeconomic difficulties were more real than monetary ones. Potted versions of Keynesian theory understandably came to focus on those of its aspects that are relatively easy to build into models—the consumption function, the savings gap to be filled by investment, the multiplier, and various interest elasticities or inelasticities—rather than on the shapeless topic of hesitant and changeable expectations.

Alan Coddington [1976, in Wood 1983, IV, p. 227] commented aptly on Clower's suggestion that Keynes must have had the dual-decision hypothesis, in particular, 'at the back of his mind':

'The picture here seems to be one of Keynes with a mind full of ideas, *some* of which he got onto the pages of the *General Theory*, the task being to work out what the remainder must have been.

This is a problem of reading not so much between the lines as off the edge of the page'.

(Early reviews and anniversary reviews of the *General Theory* collected in the volumes edited by Wood, especially volume II, provide little or no support for the Clower-Leijonhufvud interpretation. More recent dissenters from that interpretation, in articles also collected in Wood's volumes, include Ivan Johnson, Robin Jackman, and Victoria Chick.)

The distinctive feature of the *General Theory*, says Don Patinkin,

'is not simply its . . . concern with changes in output, but the crucial role that it assigns to such changes as an *equilibrating force* with respect to aggregate demand and supply—or, equivalently, with respect to saving and investment'.

This is 'what Keynes's theory of effective demand is all about' and what lends crucial significance to his 'fundamental psychological law' of a marginal propensity to consume less than one [Patinkin, 1975 in Wood, 1983, I, p. 493]. In letters to economists who had written major review articles on the book, Keynes not only failed to reject the interpretation that gave rise to the standard IS-LM* apparatus but even criticised reviewers who gave insufficient emphasis to its cornerstone, his theory of effective demand.

'So there is no basis for the . . . contention . . . that the message which Keynes really meant to convey with his *General Theory* has been distorted by this interpretation' [Patinkin 1981, in Wood 1983, I, pp. 607-608].

Was Keynes a Monetarist?

As a self-taught Keynesian who had read and re-read the *General Theory* before taking any college courses in economics, and also as a self-taught monetarist, I long ago was enthusiastic about the apparently monetarist aspects of Chapter 17 in particular. Later I became disillusioned. In describing the 'essential properties' that make money a prime candidate for being in excess demand and thereby causing depression, Keynes emphasises money's yield. Its liquidity advantages in excess of

* Glossary, p. 155.

carrying costs may well pose a target rate of return that new capital goods could not match, in the view of potential investors. As a result, investment may be inadequate to fill the savings gap. Keynes even considers whether assets other than money, such as land or mortgages, might pose the same sort of troublesomely high target rate of return. He does not perceive the special snarl that results when the thing in excess demand is the medium of exchange, so that the supply of some goods and services can fail to constitute demand for others. He does not perceive the closely related difficulty that money, alone among all assets, has no price of its own and no market of its own. Keynes's context offered him an inviting opportunity to make Clower's point [1967], if he really had it in mind, about a possible hiatus between sales and purchases involving the one thing used in practically all transactions; yet he did not seize that opportunity.[2]

Keynes is not entirely consistent with himself throughout the *General Theory*, but on the whole the book conveys a real, non-monetary, theory of macro-economic disorder. It *diverted* economic research and policy away from monetary disequilibrium theory.

Disequilibrium Theory Again

That (sounder) theory can explain the consequences of imbalances between demand for and supply of money when prices and wages are not sufficiently flexible promptly to absorb the full impact of a monetary disturbance. It recognises the utter reasonableness of that inflexibility from the standpoint of individual price-setters and wage negotiators. Although myriad prices and wages are interdependent, they are necessarily set and adjusted piecemeal in a roundabout process. Whether a contemplated transaction can take place to the advantage of both potential parties may well depend on prices besides those subject to the decisions of those parties.

H. J. Davenport, to mention just one example from early-20th-century America, emphasised the monetary nature of depression.

[2] For further argument that Keynes was preoccupied with over-saving as such rather than with excess demand for holdings of money, Greidanus [1950, especially pp. 202-203].

'It remains difficult to find a market for products, simply because each producer is attempting a feat which must in the average be an impossibility—the selling of goods to others without a corresponding buying from others. ... [T]he prevailing emphasis is upon money, not as intermediate for present purposes, but as a commodity to be kept. ... [T]he psychology of the time stresses not the goods to be exchanged through the intermediary commodity, but the commodity itself. The halfway house becomes a house of stopping. ... Or to put the case in still another way: the situation is one of withdrawal of a large part of the money supply at the existing level of prices; it is a change of the entire demand schedule of money against goods' [1913, pp. 319-20].

Davenport also recognised (p. 299) that the depression would be milder and shorter if prices could fall evenly all along the line. In reality, however, not all prices fall with equal speed. Wages fall only slowly and with painful struggle, and entrepreneurs may be caught in a cost-price squeeze. Existing nominal indebtedness also poses resistance to adjustment.[3]

Monetary disequilibrium theory not only has a long and venerable history but was at times the dominant view on macro-economics (cf. Warburton's writings). Much evidence supports it, including statistical evidence of the sort that present-day monetarists produce.

Lingering Keynesianism

Unfortunately, that promising line of analysis was largely crowded out for a long time by such Keynesian concepts as the IS-LM apparatus, which for some years trivialised the confrontation between Keynesians and monetarists into supposed differences of opinion about interest elasticities. I confess that recent personal experience has made me even more weary of such concepts. While a visiting professor at George Mason University in the fall of 1983, I not only had to clean the blackboard after my classes, as a professor should; I also had to clear away what the inconsiderate professor before me had left on the board. Through the entire semester, more often than not,

[3] Further quotations from and citations to pre-Keynesian writings on the prevalence and reasonableness of price and wage stickiness can be found in my article, 'The Keynesian Diversion' [1973].

it seemed to me, what was left was the Keynesian cross diagram illustrating the simple-minded Keynesian multiplier.

I blame the Keynesians for lingering notions that government budget deficits, apart from how they are financed, unequivocally 'stimulate' the economy. Recent examples of taking this for granted are Abrams and others [1983] and Eisner and Pieper [1983]. The latter authors even argue, in effect, that partial repudiation of the US government debt through its decline in nominal market value as interest rates rise, and then through erosion of the dollar itself, should count as a kind of government revenue, making the *real* budget deficit and its real stimulatory effect slighter than they superficially appear to be.

Buchanan and Wagner [1977] argue that the Keynesian justification of budget deficits in specific circumstances has been illegitimately extended by politicians into a reason for complacency about deficits even in a much-widened range of circumstances.

'Although Keynes advocated government deficits to boost total spending in a slack economy, he also called for government surpluses to restrain inflation during booms. But politicians have selectively recalled their Keynesian theory, perennially invoking the spending rationale while conveniently ignoring the restraint Keynes envisioned' [Bendt, 1984, p. 5].

Perhaps, as is often said, Keynes was over-confident of his ability to turn public opinion and policy choices around when his own assessments changed.[4]

Over-reaction and Label-shifting

I conjecture that Keynesianism, followed by disillusionment with it, has provoked an intellectual over-reaction. I refer to doctrines of 'equilibrium always', which tend to be associated

---

[4] Professor Hayek recounted just such an expression by Keynes of his belief in his powers of persuasion in a conversation they had 'a few weeks before his [Keynes's] death'. (In 'Personal Recollections of Keynes and the "Keynesian Revolution",' *The Oriental Economist*, January 1966, reprinted in *A Tiger by the Tail*, Hobart Paperback 4, IEA, 1972, second edition 1978, p. 103).

with the rational-expectations or New Classical school, and which treat disequilibrium theories with scorn.[5] Why should stickinesses persist and contracts go unrevised, obstructing exchanges, when rational market participants would adjust prices promptly and completely to levels at which mutually advantageous transactions could proceed? Equilibrium-always theorists do not see fluctuations in output and employment as reflecting changing degrees of disequilibrium. They suggest, instead, that markets are still clearing, but with transactors sometimes responding to distorted or misperceived prices. Perceptions of relative prices and relative wages are likely to go awry when price inflation occurs at an unexpectedly high or unexpectedly low rate. In the sense that workers and producers are still operating 'on their supply curves', equilibrium, though distorted, continues to prevail. Even this distortion would supposedly be absent if people fully expected and allowed for the underlying changes in monetary policy, as self-interest would lead them to do to the extent that is cost-effectively possible.

Exaggerated notions of how nearly perfect markets are possess a strange appeal for some theorists. Anyway, these exaggerations, together with the exegetical writings of Clower and Leijonhufvud, have given perceptive Keynesians an opportunity to shift their ground gracefully, with an ironic result: something like the venerable monetary-disequilibrium theory, which Keynesianism had crowded out, now finds itself labelled 'Keynesian' by leaders in the over-reaction. The very title, 'Second Thoughts on Keynesian Economics', of an article by Robert Barro [1979], a recanted disequilibrium theorist, suggests the apparent notion that theories invoking wage and price stickiness are Keynesian.[6] Kenneth Arrow [1980, p. 149] casually refers to 'Disequilibrium theorists, . . . stemming from Keynes. . . .' Stanley Fischer (in Fischer [1980, p. 223]) refers to 'Keynesian disequilibrium analysis'. James Tobin [1980a, p. 789] refers to 'the Keynesian message' as dealing with disequilibrium and sluggishness of adjustment.

---

[5] Lucas [1975 and 1980], Lucas and Sargent [1978], and Willes [1980] are examples of writings to this effect. Comments interpreting such writings pretty much as I do include Arrow [1980], Buiter [1980], and Tobin [1980a and 1980b].

[6] Also Barro [1984, especially Ch. 19].

Frank Hahn [1980, p. 137] notes 'the present theoretical dis-illusionment with Keynes' (which, he conjectures, will be reversed). Arthur Okun's posthumous book [1981] spelling out much of the logic of price and wage stickiness is widely regarded as Keynesian. In a new textbook, Hall and Taylor [1986, pp. 13-14, 325] report that

'Keynes's idea was to look at what would happen if prices were "sticky". .... Macro-economic models that assume flexible prices and wages bear the name *classical*, because it was this assumption that was used by the classical economists of the early twentieth century. ... In the 1930s, John Maynard Keynes began to em-phasise the importance of wage and price rigidities'.

Really! A manuscript once sent me by the authors even referred to the elasticities approach to balance-of-payments analysis as Keynesian.

Among advanced thinkers, or leaders in the over-reaction, 'Keynesian' apparently serves as a loose synonym for out-of-fashion and therefore wrong. More generally, though, Keynes enjoys automatic charity. It is widely taken for granted that such a thing as Keynesian economics exists and makes sense. Discussion concerns just what it is to which the label 'Keynesian' properly applies. Pro- and anti-Keynesians alike could well use better care in the application of labels and more respect for the history of thought.

Keynes's Lasting Appeal

I do not want to seem too negative. Much can be said in Keynes's favour. He actively pursued interests in the arts, public service, and many other fields. He made contributions in analysing Indian currency and finance, in assessing economic conditions and the peace settlements after World War I, in probability theory, and in the study of monetary history and institutions. He wrote charming biographical and other essays. His contributions in the *Tract* of 1923 ran soundly along lines later called monetarist. Despite unintended influences that his later doctrines may have had, Keynes himself was a lifelong and eloquent opponent of inflation [Humphrey, 1981].

Here, however, our concern is mainly with the *General Theory*. In writing it, Keynes was no doubt moved by a benevolent,

if perhaps patrician, humanitarianism—he meant well. Assuming that a first-best (monetarist) diagnosis of and policy
response to the depression of the 1930s was somehow not in
the cards, then the policies seemingly recommended by the
General Theory would have been a good second-best approach.
In the United States, however, what brought recovery was not
policies inspired by Keynes but an almost accidental monetary
expansion, unfortunately interrupted in 1936-37, and finally
wartime monetary expansion. The ideas of the *General Theory*
took several years to filter down through the academic world
and did not gain major influence in the policy arena until
after the war. Those policy ideas may well have been beneficial
in the short run, but their long-run harmfulness started becoming evident in the 1960s, and more so in the 1970s.

Why, even today, after so much academic dissection of
Keynesian ideas and so much sorry experience with their
results in practice, does the Keynes of the *General Theory*
remain for many a fascinating and even heroic figure? The
disorganisation, obscurities, and contradictions of the book,
together with its apparent profundity and novelty, actually
keep drawing attention to it.[7] Writing in 1946 (in Wood [1983,
II, p. 193]), Paul Samuelson found it

> 'not unlikely that future historians of economic thought will
> conclude that the very obscurity and polemical character of the
> *General Theory* ultimately served to maximize its long-run
> influence'.

Different economists can read their own favourite ideas into
the *General Theory*. Left-wingers, delighted to learn that no
mechanism exists to keep saving and investment equal at full
employment, can use that supposed fundamental flaw as one
more stick to beat the capitalist system with. Right-wing
Keynesians (e.g., Polanyi [1948]) rejoice that an easy repair
will preserve and strengthen the system.

James Schlesinger [1956, in Wood 1983, II, p. 281] suggested
that what makes Keynes so satisfying is not his theoretical
structure but his 'emotional attractiveness'. For many econ-

---

[7] Although I am not directly acquainted with the James Joyce industry, I suspect
that *Ulysses* and the *General Theory* are alike in offering employment for academic
labourers of a certain kind. My own admittedly lame excuse is that I have never
written on Keynes except by invitation.

omists whose views were shaped by the events of the 1930s, he 'represents the Proper Attitude Toward Social Problems'. For them,

> 'the symbolic Keynes will retain his present position of veneration, for he is the continuing embodiment of the Dreams of Their Youth—the reforming fervor of ancient days'.

Appraisal

The discussions, research, and attitudes evoked by the *General Theory* offer much to admire. Even as propaganda for a short-run policy stance, the book may have had merit (as I said above, with heavy qualifications). But does it deserve lasting admiration as a scientific performance? Even from students writing examination papers under time constraint and stress, we teachers expect adequately clear exposition; and a student's protests about 'what he meant . . .'—about what was 'at the back of his mind', to adopt a phrase from Keynes's sympathetic interpreters—do not suffice to get his grade revised upward. Keynes, likewise, hardly deserves credit for what he supposedly may have meant but did not know how to say. If, more than 50 years later, scholars are still disputing the central message of the *General Theory*, that very fact should count against rather than in favour of Keynes's claim to scientific stature. Whatever the *General Theory* was, it was not great science. It was largely a dressing-up of old fallacies. Worse, for many years it crowded better science off the intellectual scene.

If Keynes had never written, I conjecture, experience in the Great Depression would have prodded economists towards rediscovering and perfecting monetary $=$ disequilibrium theory. Researchers like Clark Warburton would have gained respectful attention earlier. Whatever one may say favourably about Keynes's work, it did divert attention away from theories that stand up better to factual experience and critical inspection.

REFERENCES

Abrams, Richard K., Richard Froyen, and Roger N. Waud [1983]: 'The State of the Federal Budget and the State of the Economy', *Economic Inquiry*, 21, October, pp. 485-503.

Arrow, Kenneth J. [1980]: 'Real and Nominal Magnitudes in Economics', *The Public Interest*, Special Issue, pp. 139-150.

Barro, Robert J. [1979]: 'Second Thoughts on Keynesian Economics', *American Economic Review*, 69, May, pp. 54-59.

Barro, Robert J. [1984]: *Macroeconomics*, New York: Wiley.

Bendt, Douglas L. [1984]: 'Leashing Federal Spending', *The Chase Economic Observer*, 4, March/April, pp. 3-5.

Brockway, George P. [1986]: 'Choking to Death on Cream', *New Leader*, 69, 27 January, pp. 12-13.

Buchanan, James M., and Richard E. Wagner [1977]: *Democracy In Deficit: The Political Legacy of Lord Keynes*, New York: Academic Press.

Buiter, Willem [1980]: 'The Macroeconomics of Dr Pangloss: A Critical Survey of the New Classical Macroeconomics', *Economic Journal*, 90, March, pp. 34-50.

Christiernin, Pehr Niclas [1761]: *Summary of Lectures on the High Price of Foreign Exchange in Sweden*, trans. by Robert V. Eagly as pp. 41-99 of Eagly's *The Swedish Bullionist Controversy*, Philadelphia: American Philosophical Society, 1971.

Clower, Robert W. [1965]: 'The Keynesian Counterrevolution: A Theoretical Appraisal', in F. H. Hahn and F. P. R. Brechling (eds.), *The Theory of Interest Rates*, London: Macmillan, pp. 103-125.

Clower, Robert W. [1967]: 'A Reconsideration of the Microfoundations of Monetary Theory', *Western Economic Journal*, 6, December, pp. 1-9.

Davenport, Herbert Joseph [1913]: *The Economics of Enterprise*, New York: Macmillan.

42   KEYNES'S GENERAL THEORY: FIFTY YEARS ON

Davis, J. Ronnie [1971]: *The New Economics and the Old Economists*, Ames: Iowa State University Press.

Dorfman, Joseph [1959]: *The Economic Mind in American Civilization*, Vol. 5, New York: Viking Press.

Eisner, Robert, and Paul J. Pieper [1984]: 'A New View of the Federal Debt and Budget Deficits', *American Economic Review*, 74, March, pp. 11-29.

Fischer, Stanley (ed.) [1980]: *Rational Expectations and Economic Policy*, Chicago: University of Chicago Press for NBER.

Glazier, Evelyn Marr [1970]: *Theories of Disequilibrium: Clower and Leijonhufvud Compared to Hutt*, University of Virginia Master's thesis.

Greidanus, Tjardus [1950]: *The Value of Money*, 2nd edn., London: Staples Press.

Grossman, Herschel I. [1972]: 'Was Keynes a "Keynesian"? A Review Article', *Journal of Economic Literature*, 10, March, pp. 26-30 (reprinted in Wood 1983, III, pp. 479-85).

Hahn, Frank [1980]: 'General Equilibrium Theory', *The Public Interest*, special issue, pp. 123-38.

Hall, Robert E. and John B. Taylor [1986]: *Macroeconomics*, New York: Norton.

Hume, David, 'Of Money' [1752]: reprinted in Eugene Rotwein (ed.), *Writings on Economics*, Madison: University of Wisconsin Press, 1970, pp. 33-46.

Humphrey, Thomas M. [1981]: 'Keynes on Inflation', Federal Reserve Bank of Richmond *Economic Review*, 67, January/February, pp. 3-13.

Hutt, W. H. [1963]: *Keynesianism—Retrospect and Prospect*, Chicago: Regnery.

Hutt, W. H. [1974]: *A Rehabilitation of Say's Law*, Athens: Ohio University Press.

Hutt, W. H. [1979]: *The Keynesian Episode: A Reassessment*, Indianapolis: Liberty Press.

Johnson, Harry G. [1971]: 'The Keynesian Revolution and the Monetarist Counter-Revolution', *American Economic Review*, 61, May, pp. 1-14.

Keynes, John Maynard [1936]: *The General Theory of Employment, Interest and Money*, London: Macmillan and New York: Harcourt, Brace.

Keynes, John Maynard [1923]: *A Tract on Monetary Reform*, London: Macmillan.

Keynes, John Maynard [1930]: *A Treatise on Money*, 2 vols., London: Macmillan.

Leijonhufvud, Axel [1968]: *On Keynesian Economics and the Economics of Keynes*, New York: Oxford University Press.

Lester, Richard A. [1939]: *Monetary Experiments: Early American and Recent Scandinavian*, Princeton: Princeton University Press, reprinted Newton Abbot, England: David & Charles Reprints, 1970.

Lucas, Robert E., Jr. [1975]: 'An Equilibrium Model of the Business Cycle', *Journal of Political Economy*, 83, December, pp. 1,113-1,144.

Lucas, Robert E., Jr. [1980]: 'Methods and Problems in Business Cycle Theory', *Journal of Money, Credit, and Banking*, 12, November, Part 2, pp. 696-715.

Lucas, Robert E., Jr., and Thomas J. Sargent [1978]: 'After Keynesian Macroeconomics', in *After the Phillips Curve: Persistence of High Inflation and High Unemployment*, Boston: Federal Reserve Bank of Boston, pp. 49-72.

Meltzer, Allan H. [1981]: 'Keynes's *General Theory*: A Different Perspective', *Journal of Economic Literature*, 19, March, pp. 34-64.

Meltzer, Allan H. [1983]: 'Interpreting Keynes', *Journal of Economic Literature*, 21, March, pp. 66-78.

Okun, Arthur [1981]: *Prices and Quantities*, Washington: Brookings Institution.

Polanyi, Michael [1948]: *Full Employment and Free Trade*, Cambridge: Cambridge University Press.

Tobin, James [1980a]: 'Are New Classical Models Plausible Enough to Guide Policy?', *Journal of Money, Credit, and Banking*, 12, November 1980, Part 2, pp. 788-99.

Tobin, James [1980b]: *Asset Accumulation and Economic Activity*, Oxford: Basil Blackwell.

Warburton, Clark [1966]: *Depression, Inflation, and Monetary Policy*, Baltimore: Johns Hopkins Press.

Warburton, Clark [1981]: 'Monetary Disequilibrium Theory in the First Half of the Twentieth Century', *History of Political Economy*, Vol. 13, Summer, pp. 285-99.

Warburton, Clark, book-length manuscript on the history of monetary = disequilibrium theory, available in the library of George Mason University, Fairfax, Virginia.

Willes, Mark H. [1980]: ' "Rational Expectations" as a Counterrevolution', *The Public Interest*, Special Issue, pp. 81-96.

Wood, John Cunningham (ed.) [1983]: *John Maynard Keynes: Critical Assessments*, 4 vols., London: Croom Helm. (Contains, among other items, Victoria Chick [1978], 'The Nature of the Keynesian Revolution: A Reassessment', IV, pp. 293-314; A. Coddington [1976], 'Keynesian Economics: The Search for First Principles', IV, pp. 216-34; H. I. Grossman [1972], 'Was Keynes a "Keynesian"? A Review Article', III, pp. 479-85); W. H. Hutt [1965], 'Keynesian Revisions', III, pp. 402-15; R. Jackman [1974], 'Keynes and Leijonhufvud', IV, pp. 31-43; I. C. Johnson [1978], 'A Revised Perspective of Keynes's General Theory', II, pp. 381-99; Don Patinkin [1975], 'The Collected Writings of John Maynard Keynes: From the *Tract* to the *General Theory*', I, pp. 487-509; Don Patinkin [1981], 'New Materials on the Development of Keynes's Monetary Thought', I, pp. 590-613; P. Samuelson [1946], 'Lord Keynes and *The General Theory*', II, pp. 190-202; James Schlesinger [1956], 'After Twenty Years: The General Theory', II, pp. 266-85.)

Yeager, Leland B. [1973]: 'The Keynesian Diversion', *Western Economic Journal*, 11, June, pp. 150-63.

2. Keynes's Political Legacy*

MILTON FRIEDMAN

Nobel Laureate 1976

*This essay is adapted from Professor Friedman's comments at one of the sessions of a meeting of The Mont Pélèrin Society held at Cambridge, England, in 1984.

Milton Friedman

MILTON FRIEDMAN was born in 1912 in New York City and graduated from Rutgers before taking an MA at Chicago and a PhD at Columbia. From 1935-37 he worked for the US National Resources Committee, from 1937-40 for the National Bureau of Economic Research, and from 1941-43 for the US Treasury. From 1946 to 1977 he taught at the University of Chicago, where in 1962 he became the Paul Snowden Russell Distinguished Service Professor of Economics.

Milton Friedman is now a Senior Research Fellow at the Hoover Institution of Stanford University. He has taught at universities throughout the world, from Cambridge to Tokyo. Since 1946 he has also been on the research staff of the National Bureau of Economic Research. Professor Friedman was awarded the 1976 Nobel Prize in Economic Sciences.

Among his best known books are *Essays in Positive Economics* (1953), *Studies in the Quantity Theory of Money* (ed., 1956), *A Theory of the Consumption Function* (1957), *Capitalism and Freedom* (1962), (with Anna J. Schwartz) *A Monetary History of the United States, 1867-1960* (1963), *The Optimum Quantity of Money* (1969), and (with Rose Friedman) *Free to Choose* (1980) and *The Tyranny of the Status Quo* (1984). The IEA has published his Wincott Memorial Lecture, *The Counter-Revolution in Monetary Theory* (1970), *Monetary Correction* (1974), *Unemployment versus Inflation?: An Evaluation of the Phillips Curve* (1975), *From Galbraith to Economic Freedom* (1977), and *Inflation and Unemployment: The New Dimension of Politics* (The 1976 Alfred Nobel Memorial Lecture, 1977); and his contributions to the IEA Seminar, *Inflation: Causes, Consequences, Cures* (1974), and to *The Unfinished Agenda: Essays in Honour of Arthur Seldon* (1986).

Keynes's Political Legacy

MILTON FRIEDMAN

Keynes's heritage was twofold—to technical economics and to politics. I have no doubt that Keynes's bequest to technical economics was extremely beneficial, and that historians of economic thought will continue to regard him as one of the great economists of all time, in the direct line of succession to his famous British predecessors, Adam Smith, David Ricardo, J. S. Mill, Alfred Marshall, and W. Stanley Jevons.

The situation is very different with respect to Keynes's bequest to politics, which has had far more influence on the shape of today's world than his bequest to technical economics. In particular, it has contributed substantially to the proliferation of overgrown governments, increasingly concerned with every aspect of the daily lives of their citizens.

Technical Economics

I do not exempt *The General Theory* from my judgement about Keynes's contribution to technical economics, and can best explain why by quoting from an earlier article of mine in which I defended myself from the charge by Don Patinkin and Harry Johnson that, in Patinkin's words, my 'analytical framework is Keynesian', and, in Johnson's, that my 'classic restatement of the quantity theory of money . . . is . . . essentially a generalisation of Keynes's theory of liquidity preference'.[1]

The General Theory is a great book, at once more naïve and more profound than the 'Keynesian economics' that Axel Leijonhufvud[2] contrasts with the 'economics of Keynes'. At the heart of *The General Theory* is an extremely simple hypothesis,

---

[1] Don Patinkin, 'Friedman on the Quantity Theory and Keynesian Economics', in Robert J. Gordon (ed.), *Milton Friedman's Monetary Framework*, University of Chicago Press, Chicago, 1974; Harry G. Johnson, 'The Keynesian Revolution and the Monetarist Counter-Revolution', *American Economic Review*, May 1971, p. 114.

[2] *On Keynesian Economics and the Economics of Keynes: A Study in Monetary Theory*, Oxford University Press, New York, 1968.

although, of course, it is over-simplified. But Keynes was no Walrasian seeking a general and abstract system of all-embracing simultaneous equations. He was a Marshallian, an empirical scientist seeking a simple, fruitful hypothesis.

I believe that Keynes's theory is the right kind of theory in its simplicity, its concentration on a few key magnitudes, its potential fruitfulness. I have been led to reject it, not on these grounds, but because I believe that it has been contradicted by experience.

The General Theory is profound in the wide range of problems to which Keynes applies his hypothesis, in the interpretations of the operations of modern economics and, particularly, of capital markets that are strewn throughout the book, and in the shrewd and incisive comments on the theories of his predecessors. These insights clothe the bare bones of his theory with an economic understanding that is the true mark of his greatness.

Rereading *The General Theory* has reminded me what a great economist Keynes was and how much more I sympathise with his approach and aims than with those of many of his followers.[3] Why have economists reacted so differently to *The General Theory*?

I was myself first strongly impressed with the importance of the Chicago tradition during a debate I had with Abba P. Lerner on Keynes in the late 1940s. Lerner and I were graduate students during the early 1930s, before the publication of *The General Theory*; we have a somewhat similar Talmudic cast of mind and a similar willingness to follow our analysis to its logical conclusion. These have led us to agree on a large number of issues—from flexible exchange rates to the preferability of a volunteer army. Yet we were affected quite differently by the Keynesian revolution—Lerner becoming an enthusiastic convert whilst I remained largely unaffected and, if anything, somewhat hostile.

During the course of the debate, the explanation of this difference became crystal-clear. Lerner had been trained at the London School of Economics, where the dominant view was that the depression was an inevitable result of the preceding

---

[3] This and the preceding three paragraphs adapted from my 'Comments on the Critics', in Robert J. Gordon (ed.), *op. cit.*, pp. 133-34.

boom; that it was deepened by the attempts to prevent prices and wages from falling and firms from going bankrupt; that the monetary authorities had brought on the depression by inflationary policies before the crash and had prolonged it by 'easy money' policies thereafter; that the only sound policy was to let the depression run its course, bring down money costs, and eliminate weak and unsound firms.

In contrast to this dismal picture, the news emerging from Cambridge about Keynes's interpretation of the depression and of the 'right' policy to cure it must have come like a flash of light on a dark night. It offered a far more hopeful diagnosis of the disease. More important, it offered a more immediate, less painful and more effective cure in the form of budget deficits. It is easy to see how a young, vigorous, and generous mind would have been attracted to it.

The intellectual climate at Chicago had been wholly different from that at the LSE. My teachers regarded the depression as largely the product of misguided government policy. They blamed the monetary and fiscal authorities for permitting banks to fail and the quantity of deposits to decline. Far from preaching the necessity of letting deflation and bankruptcy run their course, they issued repeated calls for government action to stem the deflation.

There was nothing in these views to repel a student, or to make Keynes attractive. On the contrary, so far as policy was concerned, Keynes had nothing to offer those of us who had sat at the feet of Simons, Mints, Knight, and Viner.[4]

Keynes's Bequest to Politics

I can best indicate what I regard to be Keynes's bequest to politics by quoting from his famous letter to Professor Hayek praising *The Road to Serfdom*. The part generally quoted is from the opening paragraph of the letter:

> 'In my opinion it is a grand book . . . [M]orally and philosophically I find myself in agreement with virtually the whole of it; and not only in agreement with it, but in deeply moved agreement'.

[4] This and the preceding four paragraphs adapted from *ibid.*, pp. 162-63.

The part I want to direct attention to comes later:

'I should therefore conclude your theme rather differently. I should say that what we want is not no planning, or even less planning, indeed I should say that we almost certainly want more. But the planning should take place in a community in which as many people as possible, both leaders and followers, wholly share your own moral position. Moderate planning will be safe if those carrying it out are rightly orientated in their own minds and hearts to the moral issue. . . .

'What we need therefore, in my opinion, is not a change in our economic programmes, which would only lead in practice to disillusion with the results of your philosophy; but perhaps even the contrary, namely, an enlargement of them. . . . No, what we need is the restoration of right moral thinking—a return to proper moral values in our social philosophy. . . . Dangerous acts can be done safely in a community which thinks and feels rightly, which would be the way to hell if they were executed by those who think and feel wrongly'.[5]

Keynes very effectively convinced a much broader group than economists of the two concepts implicit in his letter to Hayek: first, the 'public interest' concept of government; second, the concept of benevolent dictatorship—that all will be well in society if only good men are in power. Clearly, Keynes's agreement with 'virtually the whole' of *The Road to Serfdom* did not extend to the chapter entitled 'Why the Worst Get on Top'.

This chapter can itself be regarded as partly anticipating one of the most important recent developments in economics, one in which many economists, notably James Buchanan, Gordon Tullock, George Stigler and Gary Becker, amongst others, have played major roles, namely, the analysis of political entities in terms strictly parallel to the analysis of market entities—the economics of 'public choice'. That analysis treats government, civil servants, elected officials, political activists, and voters in the same way that it treats consumers, employees, and other participants in the economic market—as acting to serve their own interests, where in both cases the term 'interests' is to be interpreted broadly to include not only pecuniary but

5 Donald Moggridge (ed.), *John Maynard Keynes, The Collected Writings*, Vol. XXVII: *Activities, 1940-1946*, The Macmillan Press and Cambridge University Press for the Royal Economic Society, 1980, pp. 385, 387, 388.

non-pecuniary interests, such as an easy life, 'serving the public', gaining power, and so on in infinite variety.

Keynes's Belief in Social Engineering

Keynes believed that economists and others could best contribute to the improvement of society by investigating how to manipulate the levers actually or potentially under control of the political authorities so as to achieve ends they deemed desirable, and then persuading the supposedly benevolent civil servants and elected officials to follow their advice. The role of the voters is to elect persons with the 'right' moral values to office and let them run the country.

From the alternative, more realistic point of view, economists and other analysts can best contribute to the improvement of society by investigating what framework of political institutions will best assure that an individual government employee or elected official who, in Adam Smith's words, 'intends only his own gain . . . is . . . led by an invisible hand to promote an end that was no part of his intention',[6] and then persuading the voters that it is in their self-interest to adopt such a framework. The task is to do for the political market what Adam Smith so largely did for the economic market.

Keynes's view has been enormously influential—if only by strongly re-inforcing a pre-existing attitude in economics. Many economists have devoted their efforts to social engineering of precisely the kind Keynes engaged in, and advised others to engage in. And it is far from clear that they have been wrong to do so. It is necessary to act within the system as it is. One may regret that government has the powers it does; a classical liberal may try his best as a citizen to persuade his fellow citizens to eliminate many of those powers; but so long as they exist, it is often, though by no means always, better that they be exercised efficiently than inefficiently. Moreover, given the system for what it is, individuals may quite properly conform and promote their interests within it. Many share my view that government should neither subsidise nor operate univer-

---

[6] *The Wealth of Nations* [1776], edition edited by Edwin Cannan, Methuen, London, 5th edn., 1930, Vol. I, Book IV, Ch. II, p. 477.

sities. Yet there is surely nothing wrong in their accepting employment at state universities.

An approach that takes for granted that government employees and officials work to promote in a disinterested way what *they* regard as the public's conception of the 'general interest'—that they are acting as 'benevolent dictators'—is bound to contribute to an expansion of government intervention in the economy—regardless of the economic theory employed. A monetarist, no less than a Keynesian, interpretation of economic fluctuations can lead to a fine-tuning approach to economic policy.

Historical Experience and Keynes's Influence

The persuasiveness of Keynes's view was much enhanced in Britain by historical experience, as well as by the example Keynes himself set. Britain retains an aristocratic structure— one in which 'noblesse oblige' is more than an empty catchword. What has changed is the criteria for admission to the aristocracy—if not to a complete meritocracy, at least some way in that direction. Moreover, Britain's 19th-century *laissez-faire* policy produced a largely incorruptible civil service, with limited scope for action, but with substantial powers of decision within those limits. It also produced a citizenry which obeyed the law and was responsive to the actions of the elected officials who operated in turn under the influence of the civil service. The welfare state of the 20th century has almost completely eroded both elements of this heritage. But that was not true when Keynes was forming his views nor during most of his life.

Keynes's own experience was also influential, particularly to economists. He set an example as a brilliant scholar who participated actively and effectively in the formulation of government policy—both through influencing public opinion and as a technical expert called on by government for advice. He set an example as a public-spirited and largely disinterested participant in the political process. And it is not irrelevant that he gained worldwide fame, and a private fortune, in the process.

The situation was very different in the United States. The United States is a democratic, not an aristocratic, society, as

Alexis de Tocqueville pointed out long ago.[7] It has no tradition of an incorruptible or able civil service. Quite the contrary: the spoils system formed public attitudes far more than the supposedly non-political civil service. And it did so even after it had become very much emasculated in practice. As a result, Keynes's political bequest has been less effective in the United States than in Britain, which partly explains, I believe, why the revolution in the analysis of politics occurred in the USA. Yet even in the United States, Keynes's political bequest has been tremendously effective. Certainly most writing by economists on government policy—as opposed to scientific and technical economics—has been consistent with it. Economists have sought to discover how to manipulate the levers of power more effectively, and to persuade—or educate—government officials regarded as public-spirited to serve the public interest.

I offer my own experience as an example. Only recently have I come to the conclusion that the Federal Reserve System's imperviousness to my technical advice reflects neither the wrongness of that advice nor the ignorance of the powers that be, but rather the simple fact that the self-interest of those powers and of the Federal Reserve System would not have been served by adopting that advice. Could a system that had restricted itself to maintaining a steady and moderate rate of growth in the quantity of money conceivably have acquired the prestige and influence that the System now has? Would the head of a system that had limited itself to that modest and feasible task be regarded in poll after poll as the second most powerful person in the land?

My activities directed at criticising the 'Fed' and advising how its powers might better be exercised may not have been a complete waste of time. But their usefulness—in my present view—has been primarily to help prepare the ground for a major reform of the System rather than to improve the operation of the present System.

---

[7] A. de Tocqueville, *Democracy in America*, 2 vols., trans. Henry Reeve, ed. Francis Bowen (Boston: John Allyn, Publisher, 2nd edn., 1863). (The first French edition was published in 1835.)

Meade and Simons: Influence of Keynes

Just as Abba Lerner and I illustrate the differential influence of Keynes's technical economics, so James Meade and Henry Simons illustrate the differential influence of Keynes's political bequest on persons with similar characteristics but dissimilar backgrounds. Henry Simons had a beautifully clear and logical mind, was prepared to trust his abstract reasoning and to apply it to the real world, was a passionate egalitarian devoted to contributing to the improvement of society—admirable both intellectually and morally. Every one of these statements is equally valid for Meade. In branch after branch of policy they reached identical conclusions, yet their approach to government policy was very different. Meade, though younger than Keynes, grew up in a society that took an incorruptible civil service and a law-abiding citizenry for granted. During World War II, he worked closely with Keynes and was much influenced by him. As late as 1964, he favoured continuous 'short-run changes in monetary and budgetary policies . . . to maintain full employment'; and 'measures for the equalisation and the socialisation of property ownership . . . to supplement rather than to replace the existing welfare-state policies'.[8] This continues to be so, in modified form, today.[9]

Henry Simons, seeking the same objectives and sharing the same view of how the economy operated, became famous as the author of *A Positive Program for Laissez-Faire*. The difference, I long ago decided, was that his experience had been with the inefficient and incompetent state and federal civil service in the USA, and with the US citizenry, who are anything but automatically law-obedient.

As Aaron Director put it 38 years ago:

'Just as Lord Keynes provided a respectable foundation for the

---

[8] J. E. Meade, *Efficiency, Equality and the Ownership of Property*, Allen & Unwin, London, 1964, pp. 73-75.

[9] The modification to Professor Meade's views, which he describes as the 'New Keynesianism', is that he calls for monetary and fiscal policies to keep the flow of total money expenditures in the economy on a steady expansionary path, and for a complicated system of setting wages by boards so as to keep output and employment high. (D. Vines, J. Maciejowski and J. E. Meade, *Stagflation, Vol. 2: Demand Management*, George Allen and Unwin, London, 1983.)

adherents of collectivism, so Simons was providing a respectable foundation for the older faith of freedom and equality'.[10]

To repeat, I conclude that Keynes's political bequest has done far more harm than his economic bequest, for two reasons. First, whatever the economic analysis, benevolent dictatorship is likely sooner or later to lead to a totalitarian society. Second, Keynes's economic theories appealed to a group far broader than economists primarily because of their link to his political approach. Here again, Keynes, in his letter to Hayek, said it better than I can:

'Moderate planning will be safe if those carrying it out are rightly orientated in their own minds and hearts to the moral issue. This is in fact already true of some of them. But the curse is that there is also an important section who could almost be said to want planning not in order to enjoy its fruits but because morally they hold ideas exactly the opposite of yours [i.e., Hayek's], and wish to serve not God but the devil. Reading the *New Statesman & Nation* one sometimes feels that those who write there, while they cannot safely oppose moderate planning, are really hoping in their hearts that it will not succeed; and so prejudice more violent action. They fear that if moderate measures are sufficiently successful, this will allow a reaction in what you think the right and they think the wrong moral direction. Perhaps I do them an injustice; but perhaps I do not'.[11]

Keynes did not let this analysis prevent him from serving until his death as chairman of *The New Statesman and Nation*—presumably in the hope of influencing the moral views of its editors and writers. I regard Keynes's analysis as indicating that the key problem is not how to achieve a moral regeneration but rather how either to frustrate what Keynes regarded as 'bad morals', or to construct a political framework in which those 'bad morals' serve not only the private but also the public interest, in the same way that in the economic market private greed is converted to public service.

---

[10]Aaron Director, 'Prefatory Note', in Henry Simons, *Economic Policy for a Free Society*, University of Chicago Press, Chicago, 1948, p. v.

[11]D. Moggridge (ed.), *loc. cit.*, p. 387.

3. Keynes's Intellectual Legacy

*Fred H. Gowen Professor of Economics,
University of Rochester, New York*

Karl Brunner

KARL BRUNNER is Fred H. Gowen Professor of Economics at the Center for Research in Government Policy and Business Graduate School of Management, University of Rochester, New York, and Professor of Economics at the University of Bern, Switzerland. Editor of *The Journal of Monetary Economics* and Co-chairman of the Shadow Open Market Committee.

Keynes's Intellectual Legacy

KARL BRUNNER

To discuss the intellectual legacy of Keynes requires some consideration of his methodology and approach to policy.

I. THE METHODOLOGY

Keynes's general approach to analysis and his attempts to understand or solve problems is characterised by a specific methodology. Milton Friedman described it on various occasions as a 'Marshallian position' in contrast with a 'Walrasian attitude'. The approach is common to many of our great economists. This informal methodology emphasises the importance of comparative simplicity. It thrives on a gift for and willingness to find some felicitous simplifications. There is a clear and deliberate distinction between matters of first and of second and third order of significance. It also requires the intellectual courage not to cover one's position on all sides but to disregard matters of lesser significance. The methodological message conveyed by Keynes and many great economists thus instructs us to grope for the simplest formulation that will yield insights into the (presumed) essential structure of a problem. This pattern can be recognised both in Keynes's scholarly work and in his discussions addressed to problems of policy.

This message of simplification in Keynes's legacy is neither especially 'Keynesian' nor particularly new. But we still should recognise its importance even though it is a message that many Keynesians dismissed, and non-Keynesians reject. Much of the empirical work accumulated by Keynesians could be characterised, following Milton Friedman, as a marriage between Walras and Schmoller. The pursuit of large-scale econometric models was dominated by the idea that 'everything depends on everything else'. Indeed, everything does depend on everything else. Keynes understood, however, that *disregard-*

59

ing this injunction is a necessary condition for cognitive *progress*. Our knowledge progresses by recognising major differences in the degrees of dependence and effectively exploiting these differences in the construction of hypothesis and theory. Similarly, the approach to inflation cultivated by many Keynesians around the world offers another example. Inflation is presented as a complex sociological phenomenon deeply entrenched in the social fabric, and conditioned by a shifting and wide array of circumstances. My experiences in Europe suggest that among many European—and particularly German—economists, any simple explanation of inflation is *a priori* suspect.

Trend to 'Rigorisation'

Lastly, the trend towards 'rigorisation' (that is, one of formal models) involves two strands contrasting with Keynes's methodological message. Both strands are well expressed by adherents of rational expectation theory, for example, the Minnesota group. One strand conveys that only a full 'rigorised' formulation can be expected to offer any relevant knowledge. The second strand asserts that only formulations derived from 'first principles' can be assigned (on *a priori* grounds) any potential cognitive status. Both strands fail to recognise the fundamental importance of Keynes's methodological message, a message which has successfully guided cognitive endeavours for many years. This tradition, confirmed by Keynes, does not condemn 'rigorisation', provided it does not trade-off relevant content. But it maintains that important knowledge can and has been acquired with partially and incompletely 'rigorised' formulations. It also rejects the Cartesian fallacy of 'first principles'. There are no 'first principles' in this sense, and science actually moves in its cognitive struggle in the opposite direction. We begin with empirical problems and regularities and grope for superior hypotheses and theories. But knowledge is acquired at each stage of the process. Keynes's legacy reminds us that the new methodological 'laws' would seriously impair our cognitive struggle.

II. KEYNES'S ECONOMICS

The intellectual scenery shifts radically when we move to Keynes's economics. There is, of course, the *Tract on Monetary Reform* and *The Treatise on Money*. Both books are still worth reading today. But Keynes's economics centres on *The General Theory* and I now attend to the legacy of ideas conveyed with this book.

Two questions are frequently asked when appraising Keynes's legacy in economics: Was Keynes a great economist? And was Keynes a 'Keynesian'? In some sense he has generally been regarded as a 'Keynesian'. My subsequent comments in this and the next section should confirm this answer. No direct answer is offered to the first question. The reader may judge for himself on the basis of my comments.

Keynes was a brilliant intellectual with wide interests, an excellent writer and outstandingly articulate. He seemed to have little patience for ivory-tower exercises and his mind was always concerned with the serious and important problems of his day. His influence on developments in the profession was indeed remarkable and a rare historical event. His basic ideas permeated the thinking of professional economists and influenced much empirical work leading beyond his general framework.

But we still need to ponder this framework and the basic ideas it expresses. Persistent mass unemployment was what motivated Keynes to develop his basic theme immediately at the beginning of *The General Theory*. The market system suffers under a fatal flaw. A pervasive market failure prevents the emergence of transactions which remove the discrepancy between the marginal utility of real wages and the marginal disutility of work. The system apparently generates not enough transactions on labour markets with potentially mutually advantageous trades. Traditional price theory, paying insufficient attention to transaction and information costs, and thus to the peculiar institutions of labour markets, experiences difficulties in coping with unemployment problems. Two avenues were open to Keynes: either to cope with the incomplete state of price theory or to abandon it. For the range of labour market problems he chose the latter route. This choice influenced many Keynesians to disregard price theory, most particularly in the context of labour market problems. It also contributed, in spite of Keynes's methodological message, to the replacement of an economic analysis of inflation by diffuse sociological considerations.

The market system's failure is not confined to the labour market in Keynes's view. The vision of *The General Theory* assigns a central role to investment. This process seems to be controlled by a market—the stock market—which operates in defiance of any relevant social function. Stock prices are formed by complex attempts to guess what other people are guessing (*cf.* Keynes's 'beauty contest'[1]). The resulting pattern of stock prices cannot therefore be expected to provide any socially relevant signals for resource allocation. In contrast to the complex game of expectations on the stock market, the bond market is controlled by regressive expectations and the output or labour market apparently by extrapolative expectations.

The Low Output/Low Employment Trap

These strands of Keynes's vision, together with other building blocks, determine that the economy settles in a trap of low output and low employment. Underemployment equilibrium is, according to Keynes's vision, the fate of all modern market systems. A 'trade-cycle' moves the system around its trap of low output and employment. But this aspect was of secondary interest to Keynes. His theme assigns essentially little signifi- cance to monetary affairs with respect to both the low output trap and the trade-cycle without invoking a liquidity trap. Monetary manipulation and price-wage adjustments can only produce, at best, temporary deviations from low output with, moreover, little effect on the trade-cycle. In Keynes's vision secular stagnation is essentially a real phenomenon requiring ultimately fundamental socio-political restructuring.

The central theme of an economy trapped in low output is shared by many Keynesians. Some elaborated it into a multi-

---

[1] Described and discussed by Professor Patrick Minford in his essay, 'Expectations and the Economy', in this volume (pp. 103-104).—ED.

plicity of traps, each one stable within some specific range. But variations on the theme unavoidably developed. The emergence of the IS/LM paradigm* established a particularly important and influential variant, but this version is difficult to reconcile with the theme traced above. The distinct patterns of stock and bond markets emphasised by Keynes cannot be usefully summarised into a single non-money asset market. The IS/LM approach thus loses some crucial aspects of the underlying processes emphasised by Keynes which produce the low-level trap and also justify some of his major policy conclusions.

There was and there still is an alternative programme expressed in the classical traditions by the evolution of price and monetary theory. The programme was certainly incomplete and undeveloped at the time of the Great Depression. This experience offered a major challenge to elaborate and develop the classical research programme. Keynes responded to the challenge, however, with a new paradigm, directing the profession's attention away from a potentially useful and promising programme, which he replaced by a programme that distorted our vision and conditioned our approaches to policy-making and eventually produced serious problems. Harry Johnson predicted in the early 1970s that Keynesian theory would emerge again with rising unemployment and vanishing inflation. But Keynesian theory failed to cope adequately with *both* problems. The pervasive unemployment in contemporary Europe cannot be explained in Keynes's terms. It is approachable in terms of a classical programme kept alive by Clark Warburton in the 1940s and resurrected during the past 30 years by an increasing number of professionals. And ironically, even the Great Depression, the motivating impulse for *The General Theory*, does not require a vision of secular stagnation and of low output and employment traps controlled by fundamental real structural conditions. We find in retrospect that the renewed classical programme explains quite well both the deflation and lingering unemployment in the 1930s and the inflation with rising unemployment in the 1970s. Yeager properly cautions us in this context about over-reacting against the Keynesian alternative and the prevalent belief that 'sticky

*Glossary, p. 155.

prices' (i.e., prices not fully reflecting all continuing shocks) are something essentially Keynesian. Recognition of their occurrence and their rationale forms an essential component of classical theory.

III. POLICY AND POLITICAL ECONOMY

Keynes's influence on the public's awareness of and the profession's approach to policy reflects the influence exerted by his vision of the economic process which determined the basic structure of his conception of policy. A subtle strand of Keynes's policy thinking involves a fundamental issue in political economy, however, to be discussed below (p. 66).

Keynes advocated the joint imposition of investment control, exchange control with particular emphasis on control over capital flows, and trade controls. These three building blocks form a unified structure necessary to cope with the system's basic flaws. There was little role for monetary policy in this scheme. Fiscal policy, incorporating a direct involvement in investment expenditures, supplemented with indirect taxes and subsidies modifying private investments, was advanced as the effective instrument of investment control. Such control was immediately suggested by the failure of the market expressed in a low output trap and the socially irrelevant mode of operation of the stock market. Investment control would provide a social rationale and move the economy upwards. But investment controls were hardly sufficient, since they would be endangered by an uncontrolled exchange market. The free traffic in capital transactions had to be prohibited. Exchange controls would therefore be particularly geared on this view to potential capital flows. But exchange control of current transactions and trade controls are unavoidable supplements to cope with evasions of capital-flow controls and to reinforce investment controls on the side of goods transactions. This package of policy ideas shaped by the underlying vision makes us appreciate the comments offered by Keynes in the Preface to the German edition of *The General Theory*. He emphasised that the German social and institutional context prevailing at the time was especially well designed for an application of his basic ideas.

Keynes's Vision of Monetary Order

Keynes's long struggle during the war years to construct an international monetary order for the post-war years is also very revealing in its subtle ambiguities. His endeavours at Bretton Woods could easily be interpreted as an attempt to evolve a sytem of rules characterising a well-specified monetary order. There appear verbal passages and references which could be interpreted in this manner, but they are overshadowed, in my judgement, by a contrasting and pervasive thrust. This thrust is guided by a specific perception of the post-war problem to be confronted by Britain. He expected that a massive re-allocation of resources towards production for export would be needed to replace the foreign investments sold to pay for the war. Such extensive re-allocation required, in his judgement, many long years. Like a company with a large investment project, England during this period required financial support. Keynes was thus interested to provide substantial credit facilities and a wide range for national policy actions. This range should include an opportunity to institute exchange and trade controls whenever deemed necessary by the national government. The rules addressed or visualised by Keynes remained vague, as is clearly revealed by his ambiguous position on the discipline imposed on domestic policies by the require-ments of balance-of-payments adjustments. Jan Tumlir sum-marises the situation thus:

> 'Keynes wanted clear rules within which national authorities would be free to manoeuvre. With respect to countries within the rules, the international authority "should not wander from the international terrain". But he had already done quite a lot to ensure that the rules would be not only quite generous but not exactly clear either'.

The net thrust of Keynes's thinking worked, so it appears, to raise the discretionary power of national and international bureaucracies.

The array of detail characterising Keynes's policy views was not rigidly reflected among the 'Keynesians'. We do encounter substantial variations in ideas and emphasis. But in spite of major differences, most Keynesians would share some common perception derived from Keynes, for instance, the reservation about the market system and concern about fundamental market failure which can be overcome only with the help of a government that can be relied upon to act in the appropriate manner. Thus emerges the disposition to an essentially activist policy-making and the concentration on fiscal policy as the dominant instrument. An extension to include activist monetary policy-making occurred, at least in the USA, over the most recent years. This vision of policy-making differs radically from the conception fostered by the classical programme. In contrast to the Keynesian disposition, the latter emphasises *not* specific actions pursued by government agencies in time but addresses the nature of the institutional framework controlling market processes.

Government as Benevolent Dictator

The difference between these visions of policy can be traced to a strand of thought permeating Keynes's and Keynesian thinking. The Keynesian tradition typically attributes to government and its apparatus the attitude of a benevolent dictator. Keynes argues in particular that people of high moral fibre tend to be attracted to the government's operation. These people can be expected to act in the public's best interests. Proponents of the classical programme are more inclined to proceed from the tradition of Mandeville and Adam Smith. Under the circumstances, they view the Keynesian addiction to regard government as a potentially benevolent dictator with substantial scepticism.

Ultimately, Keynes's vision of the political economy of government, and the multi-coloured influence exerted by his perception of the economic process, together determined a broad pattern of characteristic Keynesian policy proposals. These prospects gradually dominated the attention of the public arena during the earlier phases of the post-war era. But the resurgence of the classical programme over the past 15 years effectively challenged the Keynesian vision. Irrespective of the intellectual fate of the rival contentions, the *political* outcome will not be decided, as Harry Johnson assumed, in terms of unemployment and inflation. The policy conception of the classical programme has little market value in the political process. The political process, guided by its peculiar incentive structure, finds the Keynesian perception usefully attractive for its purposes. This difference in the *political* usefulness of the two products will probably decide the *public* fate of the alternative programmes. But the longer-run consequences of the Keynesian victory in the *political* sphere may still best be analysed and understood in terms of the classical research programme.

4. Economic Events and Keynesian Ideas: The 1930s and the 1970s

MICHAEL R. DARBY

Professor of Economics,
University of California, Los Angeles

and

JAMES R. LOTHIAN

Vice President, Citicorp Investment Bank

Michael R. Darby

MICHAEL R. DARBY was born in 1945 in Dallas, Texas, and educated at Dartmouth College (AB 1967) and the University of Chicago (MA 1968, PhD 1970). In 1972 he joined the economics faculty of the University of California, Los Angeles, where he is now Professor of Economics, after a two-year stint as assistant professor at the Ohio State University. He has had visiting appointments at the National Bureau of Economic Research, of which he is currently a Research Associate, and the Hoover Institution at Stanford University. He serves as Editor of the *Journal of International Money and Finance* and on the Editorial Board of the *American Economic Review*. He is the author or co-author of seven books and monographs and of numerous professional articles on macro-economics and international finance. In June 1986, his appointment as Assistant Secretary for Economic Policy of the US Treasury was confirmed.

James R. Lothian

JAMES R. LOTHIAN is Vice President in charge of international economic research for Citicorp Investment Bank. He joined Citibank in 1972, receiving his doctorate in economics from the University of Chicago a year later. He is editor of the *Journal of International Money and Finance*, has been a Research Associate of the National Bureau of Economic Research, and has held teaching posts at Queens College of the City of New York, the University of Illinois in Chicago, and Lake Forest College. He is co-author of *The International Transmission of Inflation*, has published in numerous scholarly journals and collections and has written regularly on financial and economic topics for the business press and for business periodicals.

70

Economic Events and Keynesian Ideas: The 1930s and the 1970s

MICHAEL R. DARBY and JAMES R. LOTHIAN

Introduction

Like the proverbial chicken and the egg, economic events and macro-economic theory have borne a continuing ambiguous relationship to one another. Keynes himself, in his scathing indictment of the influence of 'academic scribblers' on policy, pointed to one such avenue of impact.[1] George Stigler [1983], in his Nobel lecture 'The Process and Progress of Economics', pointed to a channel leading in the exact opposite direction. Singling out macro-economics as 'notorious' for 'its responsiveness to contemporary events', Stigler cited the unemployment of the 1930s as the reason for the success of Keynes's *General Theory* and the inflation of the 1970s as the reason for its demise.[2]

This paper explores and develops Stigler's hypothesis. We first examine the economic experience of both the United States and the United Kingdom during the inter-war years, contrasting Keynes's perceptions of those events with the findings of subsequent empirical research. We then turn to the growing influence of Keynesian ideas on economic policy in the 1960s and 1970s, the international transmission of that influence through the Bretton Woods system, and the resultant discrediting of those ideas.

I. The Inter-War Years

To most economic observers in America at the time, the Great Depression seemed to defy explanation. Its extraordinary severity, substantial duration, and almost world-wide scope

[1] *The General Theory*, pp. 383-84.

[2] *Journal of Political Economy*, August 1983, Vol. 91, p. 534.

combined to give it the aura of an entirely new species of economic animal. For many British observers this view was reinforced by experience in the previous decade.

The Macmillan Report, published in 1931, described the 1920s in Britain as a period of 'abnormal industrial depression and extensive unemployment'.[3] Other accounts paint an equally bleak picture of those years, from Orwell's classic narrative, *The Road to Wigan Pier* [1937] to the more workaday annual summaries of the *Economist*. And even though more recent analyses of movements in aggregate income place the decade in a somewhat better light, it was by no means an ordinary period.

From the beginning of 1920 to the end of 1929, there were three full cyclical contractions and the start of a fourth, the Great Depression—constituting an historical record.[4] More-over, these four contractions, taken *in toto*, added up to seven years of business decline in the 13 years ending in 1932—another historical first. Unemployment throughout this period continually ran high, at an average rate for the years 1921 to 1929 of over 9·0 per cent, with a peak in 1921 above 12·0 per cent, a decrease of close to 5 percentage points between then and 1927, and finally a sprint to a record 17 per cent in 1932.

In the United States the 1920s, though also beginning with a severe business downturn in 1920-21, were a period of strong real growth and low average unemployment. Not until 1929 did things turn sour, but they then turned sour indeed. When the Great Depression ended in the United States in 1933, real income was nearly 45 per cent below its 1929 level and the level of unemployment stood above 20·0 per cent.

---

[3] Committee on Finance and Industry [1931], *Report*, Cmd. 389, p. 6.

[4] Sources of the inter-war data reported here and below were as follows: reference cycle dates: Arthur F. Burns and Wesley C. Mitchell [1946]; real income (net national product) for both countries and yearly UK money supply (M2): Milton Friedman and Anna J. Schwartz [1982]; UK industrial production and unemployment (as a percentage of total employees): C. H. Feinstein [1972]; monthly US money supply (M2) and the monetary base (high-powered money): Friedman and Schwartz [1963]; US industrial production: US Department of Commerce [1973]; US unemployment: Darby [1976]. Note that all per-centage changes referred to below were computed on a continuously compounded basis.

Pre-Keynesian Monetary Theory

Pre-Keynesian monetary theory had two major concerns. One, the long-run relationship between money and the price level—the 'neutrality' of money—is well known. The other, often overlooked but no less central, was the question of the dynamic process by which monetary disturbances were transmitted to prices, output and employment in the shorter run. Figuring prominently in the expositions of 18th- and early 19th-century British writers such as David Hume and Henry Thornton prior to the rebirth of the quantity theory in the latter half of this century, this question received its fullest treatment in the work of the American economist Irving Fisher, who in 1926 undertook a statistical study of US cyclical fluctuations the like of which did not become common in the literature until 40 years later.[5]

This developed schema of analysis was, however, abandoned—particularly in Cambridge, England—with little more than a nod to the empirical evidence. Assertions, by officials of the Federal Reserve System in the United States and of the central banks of other countries, that monetary policy was loose but ineffectual and the low financial market interest rates of the Depression years appear to have been the only evidence taken into account.[6] Keynes's *General Theory* can be seen as his explanation of why monetary ease did not work and what—if not money—caused the Great Depression. Fisher had proclaimed the business cycle 'a dance of the dollar'. Keynes declared it a dance of investment.[7]

With both real government spending and real consumer

[5] Fisher investigated the effects of changes in the price level on output using an empirically based version of the modern Lucas supply function.

The early pre-Keynesian analysis is typified by David Hume's 'Of Money' [1752], reprinted in Eugene Rotwein (ed.), *David Hume: Writings on Economics* [1970] and Henry Thornton, *An Enquiry into the Nature and Effects of the Paper Credit of Great Britain* [1802], ed. F. A. von Hayek [1965].

A. Robert Nobay and Harry G. Johnson [1977, pp. 471-76] have an excellent discussion of the thrust of pre-Keynesian monetary theory and its emphasis on the dynamics of the 'transition period'.

[6] Clark Warburton [1951] details (especially in his note 10) the apparent ignorance of an astonishingly large number of prominent economists of the period to the factual evidence on changes in the money supply in the 1920s and 1930s.

[7] This characterisation is taken from a lecture by Milton Friedman.

spending relatively stable in magnitude over the course of the trade cycle, investment is the component of aggregate real income that accounts for most of its cyclical variation. The pre-Keynesian monetary theory we have just reviewed and the modern quantity theory of money explain this cyclical variation in investment as a movement along a stable demand function in which expectations play a crucial but predictable (endogenous) role in the transmission of (predominantly) monetary disturbances. Keynes expected lower interest rates to increase investment in the Depression. When the increase did not occur, he concluded that an overwhelming shift in the demand curve itself must have taken place.

Keynes Confused Nominal and Real Interest Rates

The conclusion, however, did not follow. Underlying it was a confusion between Fisher's (and Thornton's) distinction between nominal and real rates of interest. Real investment is a function of real rates of interest, not of nominal rates. The latter were certainly low in the Depression but price levels in both America and Britain were falling. Real interest rates, the difference between nominal rates and the rates of inflation that investors anticipate will prevail over the lives of the particular instruments, must almost certainly have been high.

This failure to distinguish between nominal and real interest rates also led Keynes to accept the characterisation of monetary policy as loose but ineffective.[8] Keynes rationalised this alleged ineffectiveness of monetary policy by the notion of a liquidity trap. At low levels of interest rates, Keynes hypothesised, money and bonds would be near-perfect substitutes. An open-market purchase, therefore, would simply give rise to a substitution of bonds for money. Nothing else would happen. Monetary policy under these circumstances would be impotent.

Keynes explicitly stated that this 'liquidity trap' was a limiting case—one that was not known ever to have occurred in practice.[9] Nevertheless, he went on to treat it as true to a

---

[8] This same confusion is present in Peter Temin's [1976] attempt to resuscitate Keynes's explanation of the Depression. For a further critique of Temin's analysis, Arthur E. Gandolfi and James R. Lothian [1977].

[9] *The General Theory*, p. 207.

first approximation. The economic variables in his model Keynes defined in terms of wage units. Given Keynes's related assumption of a fairly stable ratio between the level of product prices and the level of wages, the overall price level, which in the classical quantity theory was the outcome of the interaction between the supply of and the demand for money, was implicitly held constant.

This set of assumptions, as it has turned out, was untenable— the 'facts' of the situation that Keynes apparently took as given were not facts at all. One of the major contributions of Milton Friedman's and Anna J. Schwartz's *A Monetary History of the United States, 1867-1960* [1963] was to explode forever this myth of an expansionary yet ineffective monetary policy in the United States. Their data show that the supply of money in the USA in the 1930s, far from increasing, fell by an unprecedented amount, slightly over 40 per cent between 1929 and 1933. The only other period in which a near-similar decline in the US money stock has been recorded was 1839-43, when M2 fell by close to 28 per cent.[10] This, too, was called a 'great depression'.

Inept US Monetary Policy in 1930s

The reason the Great Depression of the 1930s was so severe, Friedman and Schwartz concluded, was that monetary policy in the USA was so inept. Confronted by a series of bank failures that were causing substantial declines in the stock of money, the Federal Reserve took virtually no offsetting actions. Their own monetary liabilities (high-powered money or the monetary base) actually declined by 3 per cent between 1921 and 1930 and from 1930 until 1932 rose by only a little over 10 per cent. This passivity came at a time of banking panics and resultant frantic scrambles for currency by money-holders and for reserves by banks. It was as if the history of the Bank of England's actions in the 19th century in times of financial crisis had never been known and Bagehot had never written.

Analyses since then have served only to buttress the conclusions of Freidman and Schwartz. Investigations of money

[10]The figures cited are from Wallace E. Huffman and Lothian [1984].

demand behaviour have uncovered no evidence of a liquidity trap in either the aggregate time-series data or the richer cross-state data for the United States.[11] Other studies have shown that, given the greater decline in money supply in the Depression, the decline in US nominal income was in line with historical experience during other cyclical contractions.[12] In a similar vein, Darby and Michael Melvin [1986, pp. 374-84], like Clark Warburton much earlier [1951], emphasise the substantial reduction in money growth beginning in April 1928, long before the downturn in business activity in the summer of 1929, which was the result of a conscious restrictive decision of the Federal Reserve System.

A related argument, that money supply in the Depression was purely passive, responding to, rather than exerting an independent influence on, real output, has also been shown of dubious validity. Two studies examining the data for other contractionary episodes in both the USA and the UK have concluded that banking panics—the mechanism by which such induced changes in money supply supposedly occurred— were not primarily a response to the cycle.[13] These studies show further that a strong association between financial panics and marked cyclical contractions exists only when the fluctuations in money supply were themselves substantial.

Influence of the Gold Standard

A final body of evidence is provided by international comparisons. Countries like Spain and China which were not on the gold standard and, hence, were immune to the direct monetary effects of the decline in the US money supply,

[11]Gandolfi [1974] and Gandolfi and Lothian [1976] contain estimates of money demand functions from cross-state data. Meltzer [1963] and Friedman and Schwartz [1982] provide estimates from time-series data for the United States and for the United States and the United Kingdom, respectively. None of these studies shows a liquidity trap to be characteristic of the data.

[12]Lothian [1981] for estimates of one such relationship; also the discussion in Schwartz [1982].

[13]Phillip Cagan [1965] analyses the relationships among cyclical contractions, monetary contractions and financial crises for the United States during the late 19th and early 20th centuries. Huffman and Lothian [1984] make comparisons similar to Cagan's using data for both the UK and the USA for the period beginning in 1833 and ending with the Great Depression of the 1930s.

escaped the full force of the Depression.[14] Those that were on the gold standard did not. Similarly, the evidence reviewed immediately below shows that countries which left the gold standard earliest recovered the quickest.

Particularly illustrative is the inter-war experience of the UK.[15] Year-to-year, the growth of the UK money supply declined from 2·1 per cent in 1928 to 0·6 per cent in 1929 and continued at roughly the same pace in 1930 before turning slightly negative in 1931. Then, after the abandonment of gold in 1931, money supply again began to grow, increasing at a 3·5 per cent per year average rate over the next two years. Real income between 1929 and 1931 fell by nearly 8·0 per cent. At that point the recovery began, slowly at first but by 1932 gathering momentum.

In the USA during these years, money supply declined much more sharply and for a longer period than in the UK. The average decrease was 1 per cent per annum from April 1928 to April 1930, 5 per cent during the next 12 months, 20 per cent from April 1931 to April 1932, and 17·5 per cent during the next 12 months, at which time money supply growth resumed. Both real income and industrial production fell precipitously—real income by close to 35 per cent from 1929 to 1932 and industrial production by over 60 per cent. Real income in the United States, moreover, continued to fall through 1933 and, unlike the UK, failed to reach its 1929 level until almost the end of the decade.

From a cyclical standpoint, this was an exact reversal of the roles the two countries played in the previous common severe inter-war contraction of 1920-21. What makes this juxtaposition particularly interesting, for both the Great Depression and the experience of the UK in the 1920s, is that the two countries' monetary roles were also reversed. In both countries, the growth of the money supply had averaged somewhat over 12 per cent per year from 1914 until 1920. In the USA, it turned negative in 1921, then picked up substantially during the next two years and in the process more than cancelled the

---

[14]Experiences of non-gold standard countries and of countries that left the gold standard are analysed by Ehsan Choudri and Lewis Kochin [1980]. Also Irving Fisher [1936] for an earlier, and in many respects similar, analysis.

[15]This discussion draws on Lothian [1982], pp. 142-45.

1920-21 decline in the stock of money. In the UK, a monetary reversal of this sort did not take place. The money supply actually continued to decline between 1921 and 1923 after growing by less than 1 per cent in 1921. The reason for the disparity in monetary behaviour in the two countries was the desire of the British government to return to the gold standard at the 1914 parity.

The real sides of the two economies reacted as might be expected.[16] Real income and industrial production in 1921 fell in both economies by substantial amounts. But in the United States, with its post-contraction expansion in money, both measures of real activity picked up much more rapidly, and thus made up their initial declines much sooner than in the UK.

Keynes's *General Theory*, therefore, was written to explain perceived empirical paradoxes which did not exist. Contrary to contemporary impressions, monetary disturbances were of appropriate magnitude and timing to explain both the general pattern and much, though certainly not all, of the important details of the inter-war cyclical movements in America and Britain. Focussing on nominal interest rates, Keynes misdiagnosed the thrust of monetary policy and entirely missed the connection between low money growth, high real interest rates, and a low quantity of investment demanded.

II. The Post-World War II Inflation

If Keynes's model obfuscated rather than illuminated the Great Depression, its application to policy during our own era has been even more damaging. We can debate the extent to which economic ideas have consequences—whether they do in practice exert a strong independent influence on official policy or whether they merely provide rationalisations for government

---

[16]This painful process of slow monetary growth that began in 1921 and continued throughout the 1920s in the UK is one factor responsible for the high unemployment. Daniel Benjamin and Levis Kochin [1979] provide evidence of another: unemployment benefits were substantially raised in real terms, which by their calculations increased the normal (non-cyclical) level of unemployment 2 to 3 percentage points.

officials to pursue the policies they deem expedient and would have pursued in any case. But one thing is clear, the inflationary policies followed in both the UK and the USA for much of the post-war period would not have commanded the intellectual respect they did were it not for *The General Theory* and the later theorising in the same vein that it engendered.

Money, Inflation and the Keynesian Model

In the model of *The General Theory* the price level was constant. Money, therefore, was precluded from having any inflationary impact. In later versions of the model, it had no impact so long as the economy was below the level of full employment. Underlying the implementation of both sets of models, moreover, was a belief in full employment as a *desideratum*, and an emphasis on the manipulation of interest rates in the financial market as the means to achieve that goal.

The consequences of this line of reasoning were predictable and in broad outline were predicted. Inflation, said the critics of such models, would eventually rise: in one sophisticated analysis of the problem it would most likely end up rising at accelerating rates.[17]

This is, of course, what happened. In the UK, inflation started on its upward trend earlier than in the USA and ultimately reached higher peaks. Nevertheless, the basic process was the same. Money supply growth increased and inflation rose. At some juncture, the economy went into recession, whether because the monetary authorities tightened to counter-act the inflation, or because some other factors intruded, or both. For a time thereafter inflation temporally abated.

Confronted with the now lower inflation and the higher unemployment, the monetary authorities shifted gears back to expansion and thus set the next round of the process in motion. In this round, however, policy had to become more expansive than in the early stages of the previous one. The reason is that economic participants came to anticipate what was happening. They adjusted their expectations about inflation and hence

---

[17] The forecast of accelerating inflation is contained in Friedman's [1969] American Economic Association Presidential Address.

ultimately about policy. The policy stimulus to nominal spending and income had to be larger to continue to affect real income rather than simply fuelling higher prices. Thus inflation was put on an accelerating track.

Inflation in the United Kingdom in the last half of the 1950s averaged 2·1 per cent per year.[18] By the first half of the 1960s it had risen to an average annual rate of 3·6 per cent. In the United States during the late 1950s and early 1960s, in contrast, inflation was still low, averaging 1·6 per cent per year between 1955 and 1965. By the end of the decade, however, it had reached a peak of 5·2 per cent and, although falling somewhat in the aftermath of the 1969-70 recession, was soon to be heading higher. In the UK inflation continued to run a cycle ahead of the rate in the USA, moving up sharply to a peak of close to 9 per cent in 1971, before dropping back slightly a year later.

During this period, moreover, inflation became worldwide. Prices in other industrial countries followed much the same course, differing in the absolute rates of inflation, but not in their tendency to drift upwards.

At the time, the popular view among economists writing in the Keynesian tradition was that the inflation was the result of outside forces or special factors. Initially, the two most often cited were increased militancy of trade unions and spreading monopoly power of the business sector. Then in the early 1970s, when prices of agricultural products and other raw materials began to soar, proponents of this general class of explanations blamed these increases as the specific factors driving inflation. Such beliefs were confirmed by the oil-price shocks of the early and late 1970s and the further increases in inflation in the UK and the USA that came in their wake.

US Monetary Growth and World Inflation

The ability of economists who viewed the world in pre-Keynesian quantity-theory terms to project the drift of inflation during these years well before the fact is not explained. More important, the reliance on special factors runs counter to the

[18]The source of post-World War II data cited here and below is the International Monetary Fund's *International Financial Statistics*.

bulk of the empirical evidence amassed afterwards. Our own research on inflation in the United States, the United Kingdom and six other major industrial countries is a prime example.[19] The results of that study are fully consistent with the quantity-theory view.

We found the major cause of the world inflation through the early 1970s was the upward trend in American monetary growth. Through a variety of channels operating under fixed exchange rates, the expansionary policy in the USA spilled over abroad, leading to increases in monetary growth followed by inflation. Some countries, like Germany, appear to have been unwilling participants in the process. Others like the UK would have pursued expansionary policies on their own. Indeed, this divergence in goals between the United States and other countries was the major reason that the Bretton Woods system of fixed exchange rates broke down. Our researches indicated that oil-price rises in the early 1970s played a limited role.

During the late 1970s the same trend also appears to have been true. Most countries did experience a more or less similar increase in inflation following the second oil-price shock in 1979.[20] But these fluctuations in inflation rates in the various countries were around markedly different average rates of inflation for the whole period. These average rates of inflation, in turn, bore a striking correspondence to the expansiveness of policy under the prevailing floating exchange rate system. Countries that engineered a decrease in their trend rates of monetary growth during the floating-rate period relative to

[19]Darby, Lothian, *et al.* [1983], *The International Transmission of Inflation.* The other six countries analysed in that study were Canada, France, Germany, Italy, Japan and the Netherlands.

[20]The increase in annual inflation rates in the same eight countries covered in our *International Transmission* study averaged 4·9 percentage points between 1978 and 1980—the years surrounding the second oil-price shocks. Average rates of inflation in the period 1976 to 1980, however, differed substantially among these countries. Japan and Germany, the two countries with the least expansive monetary policy, experienced relatively low average rates of inflation—an average of 5·3 per cent per year for the two combined. France, Italy and the UK, the countries with the most expansive policy, experienced the highest rates—an average of 15·4 per cent per year for Italy and the UK combined and 10·4 per cent per year in France. The other three countries, Canada, the Netherlands and the USA, fell somewhere in between in terms of both policy expansiveness and inflation.

the fixed-rate period saw on average a near one-to-one decrease in their trend rates of inflation. In contrast, countries that engineered an increase in monetary growth saw on average a near one-to-one increase in the trend of inflation.[21] Oil-price increases, therefore, either generated these changes in trend monetary growth rates in the various countries, which seems implausible given the differences in their monetary institutions and policy goals, or had little substantial lasting effects.

III. CONCLUSIONS

Keynes's *General Theory* was a brilliant explanation of fundamentally misappreciated events. Subsequent research has not found evidence either of the 'loose but ineffective' monetary policy in the Depression, or of the substantial downward shift in the investment function that were central to the message of *The General Theory*. Appearances to the contrary seem to have been rooted in a major confusion between nominal and real interest rates. Had Keynes's thinking incorporated this distinction, the events of the Depression would have seemed much less paradoxical and *The General Theory* might never have been written.

Discrediting as later scholarship has been to Keynes's analysis, it is the events of the past two decades that have proved most damning. Keynes's theories were applied, but found wanting. The post-war inflation stands as their monument, a monument to an ingenious structure based upon an almost complete misinterpretation of what actually happened slightly more than half a century ago.

---

[21]Lothian [1985] for an analysis of the relationship between changes in average growth rates of money supply and in average rates of inflation in 20 OECD countries over the periods 1956 to 1973 and 1974 to 1980.

REFERENCES

Benjamin, Daniel K., and Levis A. Kochin [1979]: 'Searching for an Explanation of Unemployment in Interwar Britain', *Journal of Political Economy*, June, Vol. 87, pp. 441-78.

Burns, Arthur F., and Wesley C. Mitchell [1946]: *Measuring Business Cycles*, New York: NBER.

Cagan, Phillip [1965]: *Determinants and Effects of Changes in the Stock of Money 1875-1960*, New York: Columbia University Press for NBER.

Choudri, Ehsan U., and Levis A. Kochin [1980]: 'The Exchange Rate and the International Transmission of Business Cycle Disturbances: Some Evidence from the Great Depression', *Journal of Money, Credit and Banking*, November, Vol. 12, pp. 565-74.

Committee on Finance and Industry [1931]: *Report* (the Macmillan Report), Cmd. 389, London: HMSO.

Darby, Michael R. [1976]: 'Three-and-a-Half-Million U.S. Employees Have Been Mislaid; or, An Explanation of Unemployment, 1934-1941', *Journal of Political Economy*, February, Vol. 84, pp. 1-16.

Darby, Michael R., James R. Lothian and Arthur E. Gandolfi, Anna J. Schwartz and Alan C. Stockman [1983]: *The International Transmission of Inflation*, Chicago: University of Chicago Press for NBER.

Darby, Michael R., and Michael T. Melvin [1986]: *Intermediate Macroeconomics*, Glenview, Ill.: Scott, Foresman and Co.

The Economist, various issues, 1921-1929.

Feinstein, C. H. [1972]: *National Income Expenditures and Output of the United Kingdom, 1855-1965*, Cambridge: Cambridge University Press.

Fisher, Irving [1926]: 'A Statistical Relation between Unemployment and Price Changes', *International Labor Review*, June, Vol. 13, pp. 785-92. (Reprinted in *Journal of Political Economy*, March/April 1973, Vol. 81, pp. 496-502.)

Fisher, Irving [1935]: 'Are Booms and Depressions Transmitted Internationally Through Monetary Standards?', *Bulletin of the International Statistical Institute*, Vol. 28, pp. 1-29.

Friedman, Milton [1968]: 'The Role of Monetary Policy', *American Economic Review*, March, Vol. 58, pp. 1-17.

Friedman, Milton, and Anna J. Schwartz [1963]: *A Monetary History of the United States, 1867-1960*, Princeton: Princeton University Press for NBER.

Friedman, Milton, and Anna J. Schwartz [1982]: *Monetary Trends in the United States and the United Kingdom*, Chicago: University of Chicago Press for NBER.

Gandolfi, Arthur E. [1974]: 'Stability of the Demand for Money during the Great Contraction—1929-1933', *Journal of Political Economy*, September/October, Vol. 82, pp. 969-83.

Gandolfi, Arthur E., and James R. Lothian [1976]: 'The Demand for Money from the Great Depression to the Present', *American Economic Review*, May, Vol. 66, pp. 46-51.

Gandolfi, Arthur E., and James R. Lothian [1977]: 'Did Monetary Forces Cause the Great Depression? A Review Essay', *Journal of Money, Credit and Banking*, November, Vol. 9, pp. 679-91.

Huffman, Wallace E., and James R. Lothian [1984]: 'The Gold Standard and the Transmission of Business Cycles, 1833-1932', in Michael D. Bordo and Anna J. Schwartz (eds.), *A Retrospective on the Classical Gold Standard, 1821-1931*, Chicago: University of Chicago Press for the NBER.

Hume, David, 'Of Money' [1752]: reprinted in Eugene Rotwein (ed.), *David Hume Writings on Economics*, Madison: University of Wisconsin Press, 1970, pp. 33-46.

International Monetary Fund, *International Financial Statistics*, various issues.

Keynes, John Maynard [1936]: *The General Theory of Employment, Interest and Money*, London: Macmillan, 1967 reprint.

Lothian, James R. [1981], 'Comments on "Monetarist Interpretations of the Great Depression",' in Karl Brunner (ed.), *The Great Depression Revisited*, Boston: Martinus Nijhoff Publishing for Rochester Studies in Economics and Policy Issues, pp. 134-47.

Lothian, James R. [1985]: 'Equilibrium Relationships Between Money and Other Economic Variables', *American Economic Review*, September, Vol. 75, pp. 828-35.

Meltzer, Allan M. [1963]: 'The Demand for Money: The Evidence from the Time Series', *Journal of Political Economy*, June, Vol. 71, pp. 219-46.

Nobay, A. Robert, and Harry G. Johnson [1977]: 'Monetarism: A Historic-Theoretic Perspective', *Journal of Economic Literature*, June, Vol. 15, pp. 470-85.

Orwell, George [1937]: *The Road To Wigan Pier*, London: Victor Gollancz Ltd.

Schwartz, Anna J. [1981]: 'Understanding 1929-1933', in Karl Brunner (ed.), *The Great Depression Revisited*, Boston: Martinus Nijoff Publishing for Rochester Studies in Economics and Policy Issues.

Stigler, George [1983]: 'Nobel Lecture: The Process and Progress of Economics', *Journal of Political Economy*, August, Vol. 91, pp. 529-45.

Temin, Peter [1976]: *Did Monetary Forces Cause the Great Depression?*, New York: Norton.

Thornton, Henry [1802]: *An Enquiry into the Nature and Effects of the Paper Credit of Great Britain*, reprinted with additional material in F. A. von Hayek (ed.), London: Allen and Unwin, 1939.

United States Department of Commerce, Bureau of Economic Analysis [1973]: *Long-Term Economic Growth, 1860-1970*, Washington DC: Government Printing Office.

Warburton, Clark [1951]: 'The Misplaced Emphasis in Contemporary Business-Fluctuation Theory', in Friedrich A. Lutz and Lloyd W. Mints (eds.), *Readings in Monetary Theory*, Homewood, Ill.: Richard D. Irwin, Inc., for the American Economic Association (an expanded reprint of his article in the *Journal of Business*, 1946, Vol. 19, pp. 199-220).

5. Consumption, Savings and the Multiplier

ALAN WALTERS

Professor of Political Economy,
Johns Hopkins University, Baltimore

Alan Walters

SIR ALAN ARTHUR WALTERS has been Professor of Political Economy at the Johns Hopkins University, Baltimore, Maryland, since 1976; part-time Personal Economic Adviser to the Prime Minister since 1983 (full-time, on secondment, 1981-83). He was knighted in 1983. Born in 1926 and educated at Alderman Newton's School, Leicester, and University College, Leicester (now the University of Leicester), graduating BSc(Econ)(London) with First Class Honours in 1951; Nuffield College, Oxford (MA); Lecturer in Econometrics, University of Birmingham, 1951; Professor of Econometrics and Head of the Department of Econometrics and Social Statistics, 1961; Cassel Professor of Economics, University of London (at the LSE), 1968-76. He has held several visiting professorships/fellowships, most recently at Nuffield College, Oxford (1982-84), and the American Enterprise Institute (1983-).

Professor Walters's principal books (as author, contributor or editor) include: *Growth without Development* (1966); *The Economics of Road User Charges* (1968); *An Introduction to Econometrics* (1969, 2nd edn. 1971); *The Economics of Ocean Freight Rates* (1969); *Noise and Prices* (1974); *Microeconomic Theory* (1977); *Britain's Economic Renaissance* (1986).

Professor Walters is a Trustee of the Wincott Foundation and a former Member of the Advisory Council of the IEA, which has published his *Integration in Freight Transport* (Research Monograph 15, 1968), *Money in Boom and Slump* (Hobart Paper 44, 1969, 3rd edn. 1971), 'Land Speculator—Creator or Creature of Inflation?', in *Government and the Land* (IEA Readings No. 13, 1974), 'In Thrall to Creditors?', in *Crisis '75...?* (Occasional Paper 43, 1975), and 'The Rise and Fall of Econometrics', in *The Unfinished Agenda* (1986). He delivered the Eighth Wincott Memorial Lecture, *Economists and the British Economy* (Occasional Paper 54, 1978).

Consumption, Savings and the Multiplier
ALAN WALTERS

Of the two pillars of the *General Theory*, savings and investment, the tractability of the behaviour of consumption and savings was quite crucial. Keynes put little emphasis on the stability of private investment behaviour; he stressed the oscillations of confidence ('animal spirits', according to Joan Robinson) and the dubious role of the rate of interest and monetary policy. But the psychological propensity to consume was thought to be much more fundamental and stable.

'We are left therefore, with the conclusion that in a given situation the propensity to consume may be considered a fairly stable function.' (*General Theory*, p. 95.)

The 'Permanent Income' Hypothesis

The first studies of the consumption function appeared to confirm Keynes's conjectures. But even by the early 1940s, it was already clear that there was something wrong about them. The studies of time-series of aggregate figures for household consumption and income gave a markedly higher marginal propensity to consume (about 90 per cent in the USA and 92 per cent in the UK) than those derived from studies of family budgets for a particular year (values of *circa* 50 to 60 per cent tended to be the norm for such cross-section studies). In his momentous book, *A Theory of the Consumption Function*,[1] Milton Friedman showed that he could reconcile these results, and virtually all other evidence, by specifying that the stability was valid only for the long-run concept of 'permanent income', that is, the income one expects to receive in future years, which is, of course, closely related to total wealth including the 'human wealth' of the individual or family. Variations in income that are transitory, such as a win at the dogs, will have little effect on consumption. Friedman demonstrated that,

[1] Milton Friedman, *A Theory of the Consumption Function*, Princeton University Press, 1957.

while in the aggregate time-series the transitory components are virtually all averaged away, in the cross-section of family budgets for a particular year or month the fortuitous transitory elements are important. This spreads out incomes without a comparable spread in consumption, thus the marginal propensity to consume from the cross-section appears to be very low. Friedman showed that such appearances were deceptive and the true propensities were much higher than previously thought.

Friedman's contribution did much to offset the contemporary view, developed by Alvin Hansen and many others, that, since the propensity to save was so high and the propensity to consume so low, the capitalist system was inherently stagnant and needed large injections of government spending to maintain full employment.[2] But, more fundamentally, Friedman's ideas shifted the emphasis from short-run determinants of the life-cycle behaviour of consumer expenditure to the role of long-run influences of wealth and 'permanent' income. Keynes had recognised that wealth, and above all expectations, played important roles in business decisions, but he tended to treat the consumer as a Pavlovian dog. Friedman showed that expectations and wealth had an equally decisive influence on household spending. Households behaved rationally in a long-run sense, rather than routinely.

Empirical tests of the permanent income hypothesis (PIH) have generally failed to discredit its implications. Perhaps the most dramatic and telling test was the temporary tax increase in the United States in 1968. The federal government and much of the economics profession thought that aggregate demand was booming far too much under the stimulation of spending on Vietnam and the War on Poverty. It was thought that a temporary tax increase would cool down the overheated economy. But it had no such effect. Households and everyone else were well aware that this was merely a transitory dip in their disposable income, and, as predicted by the PIH, they maintained their spending.

---

[2] Since Friedman showed that the underlying consumption function had a marginal propensity to save which was equal to the average, thus poor and rich tended to save on the average about the same proportion of their income, this removed the argument for increasing aggregate demand by redistributing income from the rich to the poor.

The next important test of the stability and predictability of savings functions occurred when the world experienced the great inflation of the 1970s. Consumption and savings functions, at least as far as the household sector was concerned, had always been formulated as *real* relationships. They were supposedly free of money illusion; thus if all prices were doubled, one would merely double the nominal magnitudes of income, wealth, spending and savings, but the real quantities would remain the same after the event. Inflation, however, is clearly much more than such a re-labelling procedure.

The great inflation of the 1970s saw the hitherto unprecedented phenomenon of substantial and persistent negative real interest rates in virtually all Western countries. Although neither Keynes nor Friedman had given a prominent place to interest rates in their theories of saving, there was a presumption that lower real interest rates would lead to lower savings. However, this was countered by the argument that many people save in order to have a certain level of spending in their retirement, so a reduction in real interest rates may lead to an increase in savings. I believe that virtually all economists thought that, on balance, reductions in real interest rates would *reduce* savings.

Explaining Consumer Behaviour and Savings Rates

The remarkable impact on savings of the inflation and negative real interest rates, however, quite confounded all general theories of aggregate consumer behaviour. While inflation and negative real interest rates *reduced* savings rates by some 40 per cent in the United States, by 1980, the year when inflation reached its maximum, the same broad conditions gave rise to approximately a *doubling* of the savings ratio (to 15 per cent) in the United Kingdom. Outside the United States, in the rest of the OECD countries substantial increases in savings rates in the household sector took place. So far as I am aware, no-one foresaw this astonishing instability in savings rates, and efforts to explain it away *ex post* have foundered on the difficulty of accounting for the divergent behaviour of the United States and the rest of the OECD. Analysts have given up pursuing a general theory of saving and have been reduced to suggesting that the wide difference in behaviour is accounted for by the different institutional framework of the United States compared with other OECD countries, referring particularly to the tax deductibility of interest—hardly a decisive argument, I think.

One explanation that received considerable prominence in Britain during the inflation of the mid-1970s was that households had suffered a considerable erosion in the real value of their financial assets, and, in spite of negative real interest rates, made unusually large savings and sharply reduced per capita consumption in order to restore their financial assets to their usual real level. However, this proposition hardly survived the fall in inflation from 1980 to 1984 when savings rates remained remarkably high (*circa* 12-13 per cent) and financial assets rose to new records every year. Meanwhile, in the United States, in spite of tax encouragement for saving and continued high real interest rates, the savings ratio slumped to an all-time low of 4·6 per cent in 1985.

This 'maintain-your-liquid-assets' theory of consumer behaviour is a long way from both the concepts of Keynes and the felicity of Friedman's analysis. It clearly abuts on the theory of money, but in a curious way. Normally we think of the function of money and liquid assets as a sort of buffer stock to enable us to meet variations in payments as we maintain consumption. That buffer stock would be replenished normally by switching from other forms of asset holding, not by massive increases in saving. In view of such theoretical weaknesses and considering the theory's inability to account for the behaviour of the United States (and indeed the UK in the 1980s), it is remarkable that the liquid asset theory of aggregate consumer spending still has some currency in Britain.

Another approach to savings and consumption under inflationary conditions has sought the solution in a new statistical definition of income and consumption. In particular, the income of a household is defined to exclude the inflationary erosion of assets defined in money terms, such as bonds and bank deposits. In inflationary conditions, therefore, adjusted income falls much more than conventionally measured income, and so, it was thought, the stability of the consumption function would be re-established with these new definitions. In particular, it would offer a rationalisation of the fall in consumer spending and the rise in the conventional savings rate in the mid-1970s. But again, although such a re-definition can go a long way towards explaining away the mid-1970s, it failed in the period 1980-85 when rates of inflation fell some 10 percentage points and yet the savings rate remained stubbornly high.

Finally, there have been suggestions that the variation of household savings is due largely to the variations in the savings of corporations which, either directly, or indirectly through pension funds, own the businesses. When corporate savings fall, so household savings will rise to ensure that, in total, the household achieves its target savings for a rainy day or retirement. This implies that the individual saver adjusts automatically and completely to changes in corporate savings, which is extremely unlikely.

No Adequate Theory?

From all the evidence of the last 15 years, it is clear that we have no well established and adequately tested theory of the consumption function. The stability that Friedman so elegantly exposed has largely disappeared and economists have been driven to particular explanations for particular periods for particular countries.[3]

All this would be of little concern were it not for the fact that the vast and imposing edifice of Keynesian theory totters on this insubstantial foundation of the consumption function. In the familiar textbook version, the theory says that a real increase in government spending on goods and services will generate an increase of real income (GNP) of a multiple of the increase in government spending. That multiple (or the multiplier, as it is usually called) is the reciprocal of the marginal propensity to save. Thus one would find that (with all the myriad of assumptions required in such a model), if the marginal propensity to save rose, as in the mid-1970s in Britain, the multiplier would fall. And the less stability there is in the marginal propensity to save, the less a fortiori will there be in

[3] David Hendry and T. von Ungern Sternberg, 'Liquidity and Inflation Effects on Consumer Expenditure', in A. S. Deaton (ed.), *Essays in the Theory and Measurement of Consumer Expenditure*, Cambridge University Press, 1981.

the multiplier. In short, the Keynesian measures will have much more uncertain and smaller effects than expected hitherto. Let us now briefly review the views on and the values of the fiscal multipliers over the last 50 years.[4]

Multipliers of Various Kinds

There is a large number of definitions of fiscal multipliers, but all have the same broad characteristics. They reflect the expansion in output as a ratio of the fiscal expansion that is supposed to have stimulated output. The latter can take the form of the fiscal deficit (so that an increase in the deficit is expansionary), or, to be more specific, a cut in government revenue brought about by tax reductions or an increase in government spending—all measured in real terms. The multiplier with respect to government spending, for example, is the ratio of the increase in output to the increase in real government spending that stimulated the expansion. This expansionary effect occurs over a time-span. Most Keynesians appear to expect a sharp positive effect within three months, which would persist for some three or four years—after which the effects would somehow die away. But in any case such long-term residual effects were regarded as mere 'curiosa'.[5]

Most economists would agree that the effects of the Keynesian multiplier on real output and employment would be particularly potent in conditions of high and widespread unemployment. Expenditure by government, for example, would then have hardly any effect in crowding out expenditure by the private sector. And, in so far as it was considered, there would be little or no addition to inflation; prices and wages would be restrained by the surplus labour in the market. Similarly, it was thought that there would be only small leakages of such additional demand into additional net imports, so that the current balance would hardly deteriorate. By contrast, when unemployment is low, the Keynesian multiplier

[4] Much of the ensuing discussion is based on Chapters 1 to 5 of my *Britain's Economic Renaissance: Margaret Thatcher's Reforms 1979-84*, Oxford University Press, 1986.

[5] Franco Modigliani and Albert Ando, 'Impacts of Fiscal Actions on Aggregate Income and the Monetarist Controversy, Theory and Evidence', in J. Stein (ed.), *Monetarism*, North-Holland, Amsterdam, 1976, pp. 17-68.

effect on real output would be small—or at least much smaller than under conditions of mass unemployment. The main effect of an increase in government spending would be to crowd out private expenditure and to put pressure on prices and money wages, thus generating additional inflation. For a limited period additional inflation may be modified by the excess imports and reduced exports that are generated by increases in the prices of tradeable goods; but the current balance cannot go on deteriorating indefinitely; and the impact on inflation will ultimately appear.

Fortunately, at least for scientific purposes, the last 60 years or so have seen considerable variations in the extent of unemployment, fiscal deficits and government spending. These historical records have been examined by many scholars using a variety of techniques from simple comparisons of time-series of real income and measures of fiscal stance to simulations of a fiscal boost from complex econometric models. In my survey of these results I found that they were disconcertingly different from the presumptions. To summarise:

(a) the real multipliers appeared to be much larger (approximately twice as big) under condition of full employment than in times when there was high unemployment;

(b) the effect on prices was more marked during periods of unemployment whereas during full employment periods there was less inflationary effect.

These results are derived from studies of the economies of the United Kingdom and the United States covering more than a century, but because of the availability of more and increasingly accurate data, they reflect very much evidence from the years after World War II. Although many caveats must accompany any summary of statistical results, the results of studies tend to be uniform. (The most noteworthy exception comes from the Cambridge school where Messrs Featherstone and Godley continue to find fiscal multipliers as high as 3·75 in real terms.[6]) Furthermore, the results tend to confirm the common perception that, while in the fully employed 1950s and much of

6 M. Featherstone and W. Godley, 'Fiscal and Monetary Policy in an Open Economy', in Michael Artis and Marcus Miller (eds.), *Essays in Fiscal and Monetary Policy*, Institute for Fiscal Studies, Oxford, 1981.

the 1960s, the power of fiscal policy was widely recognised, in the conditions of high unemployment of the late 1970s and 1980s (recall the tenets of Butskellism and Callaghan's 'touch on the tiller'), the real fiscal multiplier seems, if anything, to be not merely much lower than in the 1950s and 1960s but even perverse and negative. For the 1970s and 1980s, fiscal deficits have had little real expansionary, perhaps even contractionary, effects and have merely added to the pressure for monetary expansion and inflation. At any rate the outcome is clear: the 1970s and 1980s have seen both a sharp increase in unemployment and more rapid inflation with reduced growth rates.[7]

Perhaps the most telling episode in the application of simple Keynesian nostrums occurred shortly after the Budget of March 1981. The fierce fiscal squeeze of that budget was condemned by 364 economists in a letter to *The Times*. In language unequivocal and extreme, the 364 said that government policy would result in prolonged decline:

> 'Present policies will deepen the depression, erode the industrial base of our economy and threaten its social and political stability.'

More or less at the same time as the 364 were appending their signatures, the economy turned into a relatively strong expansionary phase, which continued for a record period of at least five years (to 1986). The confounding of the 364's Keynesian prescription is simply one example, albeit perhaps the most interesting and amusing one, from the historical record.

These results are so much at odds with the conventional wisdom of Keynesians that they will undoubtedly provoke disbelief. Indeed, the first reaction is to ignore them. For most of the last decade or so, the standard approach has been to regard such results as beyond belief. The second reaction is to try to rationalise them away as statistical aberrations, the consequences of simplistic models, or as misconstrued econometric relationships. (Indeed, I must confess that I have been guilty of such rationalisations in my early articles in the mid-1960s.) The third-stage reaction is to accept them, at least provisionally, and to attempt to show how they fit into a longer-term, more complete analysis of multipliers.

---

[7] OECD, *Economic Outlook*, No. 38, Paris, December 1984.

One may find economists at all stages of reaction. I suspect, however, that the third-stage reaction is growing quite rapidly. In part this is because of the realisation, most painfully and pointedly demonstrated by recent federal government deficits in the United States, that fiscal expansion has to stop. I suspect that even the most avid Keynesians would not now urge additions to the fiscal deficit of the United States in the hope of promoting a reduction in unemployment from the ambient 7 per cent of 1986. Indeed, one of the most distinguished Keynesian liberals, Nobel Laureate James Tobin, has at last argued that the most important fiscal task is to bring the deficit *down*.

The Spectre of the Long Run

To some extent this is a belated realisation that the long run does exist and eventually will come back to haunt our short-run panaceas. It is true Keynes said that in the long run we are all dead—but now Keynes is dead and we are in the long run. The point is that it is simply impossible to expand the budget deficit indefinitely—or, indeed, in a non-inflationary environment, to maintain a budget deficit as a percentage of GNP which is considerably more than the rate of growth of GNP. The presumption that the private sector has an infinite appetite for gilt-edged securities and will continue to absorb issues, at the expense of other assets, in private portfolios is quite absurd. There *must* be a stop.

In the UK this 'stop' usually takes the form of a so-called 'gilt strike'. These are occasions when the Bank of England finds it virtually impossible to sell any more gilt-edged securities. Furthermore, the Bank's judgement is that even with considerable reductions in the price of gilts, few, if any, further sales would be forthcoming. It is the market's way of reminding the authorities that things have 'gone too far'.[8]

---

[8] Of course the argument has been put to the Bank that if the interest rates were increased sufficiently, that is to say, the price of gilts were brought down sufficiently low, then it would be possible to continue with the funding programme. True, but then the rise in interest rates would reap its own havoc on the viability of firms and on domestic investment programmes and so it is unlikely that the expansionary fiscal policy would in practice result in any substantial increase in real income. In fact, real income is more likely to fall, as can be illustrated by the combination of expansionary fiscal policy, funding strikes and the fall of output in 1974-75.

Expectations and the 'State of Confidence'

There is clearly something sadly wrong with the conventional conclusions of Keynesian macro-economic policy. Paradoxically, at least one tentative answer was suggested by Keynes himself in the *General Theory* (Chapter 12, pp. 148-49):

> 'The state of long-term expectations, upon which our decisions are based, does not solely depend, therefore, on the most probable forecast we can make. It also depends on the *confidence* with which we make this forecast—on how highly we rate the likelihood of our best forecast turning out quite wrong. If we expect large changes but are very uncertain as to what precise form these changes will take, then our confidence will be weak.
>
> 'The *state of confidence*, as they term it, is a matter to which practical men always pay the closest and most anxious attention. But economists have not analysed it carefully and have been content, as a rule, to discuss it in general terms. In particular it has not been made clear that its relevance to economic problems comes in through its important influence on the schedule of the marginal efficiency of capital. There are now two separate factors affecting the rate of investment, namely, the schedule of the marginal efficiency of capital and the state of confidence. The state of confidence is relevant because it is one of the major factors determining the former, which is the same thing as the investment demand schedule.
>
> 'There is, however, not much to be said about the state of confidence *a priori*. Our conclusions must mainly depend upon the actual observation of markets and business psychology.'

Economic theorists and econometricians have completely ignored this passage in the *General Theory*. Of course, confidence is difficult to define and insert in any formal abstract model and, in any case, the econometrician will find it impossible to quantify and to measure. Keynes admitted as much. Yet it is clearly a cardinal sin to confine analysis only to the clearly definable and quantifiable magnitudes, and to ignore an important determinant of behaviour simply because it cannot be encapsulated in any neat definition or be measured.

I suggest that considerations of the ambient level of confidence may take us far in rationalising the characteristics of the fiscal multipliers. Contrary to Keynes, I suspect that there is much to be said *a priori* about the state of confidence. The suggestions that follow are merely brief illustrations of the sort of considerations which should be taken seriously.

Confidence and Government Credibility

First, it seems highly likely that confidence is determined by the general *credibility* of government policy, and this will much influence the reaction of the economy to an increase in the fiscal deficit. For example, if we contrast the situation where a government increases public spending (so increasing the fiscal deficit from a surplus of minus 1 per cent of GNP to a deficit of plus 1 per cent) with another where the government increases its deficit from 7 per cent of GNP to 9 per cent, then, according to standard Keynesian analysis, the effect on real GNP, given the ambient conditions of unemployment and spare capacity, should be the same. Yet our intuition would immediately reject such a conclusion. A deficit of 7 per cent of GNP is clearly untenable (other than in conditions of continuing inflationary expropriation of the wealth of holders of money), and an increase to 9 per cent is simply not a credible policy. The budget deficit must be brought down and the increase to 9 per cent merely heralds more drastic measures, such as tax increases, expenditure reductions, interest rate increases, and so on, to be taken in the near future.

In the UK, fiscal deficits of 6 to 10 per cent, together with rates of inflation of around 14 per cent, were characteristic of much of the 1970s. Attempts at fiscal expansion, such as that of the Labour Government in 1974-75, ran quickly into the quagmire of financial crises—hardly the appropriate environment for an expansion of the real GNP. The Public Sector Borrowing Requirement (PSBR) increased from 5·8 per cent of GDP in 1973 to 9·9 per cent in 1975, and GDP *fell* by 2·5 per cent. In contrast, as we have seen, the sharp fiscal contraction of 1981 was associated with an expansion of more than 5 per cent over the next two years. The 1974 policy was destroying credibility and confidence; the 1981 budget restored credibility and established confidence.

The critical question, however, is to find a rationalisation for the association of low real multipliers with high levels of unemployment, and high multipliers with low unemployment. Again, I suspect, the concept of confidence is critical. Until 1981 in the UK, any substantial increase in unemployment usually elicited some government measures to 'return to full employment'—mainly in the form of expanded government spending to support depressed industries and areas, but also in the guise of tax reductions and additional government borrowing on the capital markets of the world. The expenditure was not merely wasteful but it also usually perverted incentives and enterprise, since the borrowing was clearly not sustainable even in the medium term without the aid of increased inflation. These are the ingredients that erode confidence, perhaps first in the capital markets, but spreading rapidly throughout the economy. From 1981, however, the régime changed. The Government reversed the normal reaction to a gathering recession. It is likely that the record of the 1980s will be very different from those of the previous three decades. The private sector is gradually adapting to the new Thatcherite régime. But it is far too soon to give any settled view of its reaction to this new environment.

All these revisions of the standard prescriptions of Keynesian doctrine are highly tentative. They are considered now by many professional economists to be no longer quite so absurd as when I originally talked about them in 1969 on the occasion of the tenth anniversary of the Radcliffe Committee Report.[9] But we have a long way to go before there is a tested and reliable model for macro-economic policy. All we can do at this stage is to post warning signs on the most serious hazards and dispel the extravagant claims which have so plagued the profession.

Finally, I suspect that Keynes would have been sympathetic to the views advanced here. He distrusted, even disliked, too much abstraction in his economics, and constantly sought verification in the markets he knew so well. The subtleties of market sentiment and psychology may elude the modeller but they should not be ignored by the economic policy-maker.

[9] *Committee on the Working of the Monetary System*, Cmnd. 827, HMSO, 1959.

6. Expectations and the Economy*

PATRICK MINFORD

*Professor of Applied Economics,
University of Liverpool*

*An earlier version of this essay appeared in *Economic Affairs*, Vol. 5, No. 2. I am
grateful to the Editors for permission to reprint it here with modifications.

Patrick Minford

A. P. L. (PATRICK) MINFORD has been Edward Gonner Professor of Applied Economics, University of Liverpool, since 1976. Formerly Visiting Hallsworth Research Fellow, University of Manchester, 1974-75. Sometime Consultant to the Ministry of Overseas Development, Ministry of Finance (Malawi), Courtaulds, Treasury, British Embassy (Washington). Editor of *National Institute Economic Review*, 1975-76. Author of *Substitution Effects, Speculation and Exchange Rate Stability* (1978), and *Unemployment—Cause and Cure* (1983), and of essays published in *Inflation in Open Economies* (1976); *The Effects of Exchange Adjustments* (1977); *On How to Cope with Britain's Trade Position* (1977); *Contemporary Economic Analysis* (1978). He contributed papers to two IEA Seminars: 'Macro-economic Controls on Government', in *The Taming of Government*, and 'Monetarism, Inflation and Economic Policy', in *Is Monetarism Enough?*. He also contributed 'Restore Market Momentum and Fight On' to *Could Do Better* (1982), and 'From Macro to Micro via Rational Expectations' to *The Unfinished Agenda* (1986).

Expectations and the Economy

PATRICK MINFORD

Keynes and the Classics on Expectations

Virtually all economic behaviour and decisions depend on the decision-maker's expectations about the future. Yet the future is unknowable, the expectations subjective; what then can an economist say constructively about them? The answer seemed to be, until quite recently: not a lot. The classical economists typically assumed either that expected future prices, etc., were the same as current prices, or that they bore some mechanical relation to them (for example, changing by *x* per cent more or less). Ironically perhaps (in view of ultimate developments), it was in fact Keynes himself who first put expectations in the centre of the economic stage with a sort of theory attached: expectations of future profit and of future interest rates are crucial to Keynes's theory of boom and slump, which still dominates modern business cycle thinking. Booms would occur when profit *expectations* were high and interest-rate *expectations* low; and vice versa for slumps. But Keynes could do little better in theorising about these expectations than to attribute profit expectations to the 'animal spirits' of business-men and interest-rate expectations to stock-market prejudice. This is, quite transparently, an evasion. Hamlet, the Prince of the drama, is a *deus ex machina*, wheeled on and off inexplicably, even arbitrarily—decidedly *not* a 'general' theory.

There is, however, one famous passage in *The General Theory* which went deeper, tantalisingly glimpsing a more persuasive theory. In it Keynes muses about the stock market and compares it to a beauty contest:

'Professional investment may be likened to those newspaper competitions in which the competitors have to pick out the six prettiest faces from a hundred photographs, the prize being awarded to the competitor whose choice most nearly corresponds to the average preferences of the competitors as a whole. . . .

'It is not a case of choosing those which, to the best of one's judgement, are really the prettiest, nor even those which average

103

opinion genuinely thinks the prettiest. We have reached the third degree where we devote our intelligence to anticipating what average opinion expects average opinion to be.' (p. 156)

Adoption of Rational Expectations

This is so near to modern rational expectations theory, and yet so far—as we shall shortly see. This passage, indeed, turns out to be Keynes's digression on the hopeless *irrationality* of expectations and how useless it is for economists to try to explain them. Some of Keynes's disciples adopted this view. Others in the 1950s modified it somewhat to allow for 'adaptiveness'. They argued that expectations, wherever they originated (in irrational prejudices, animal spirits, etc.) would gradually be modified in the light of forecast errors; the result was that expectations, for example, of inflation, would gradually tend towards actual inflation if the situation remained unchanged for long enough, because people would *learn from their experience*.

This expectations theory was a distinct improvement on its predecessors, since it recognised that people learn systematically and that this applies to expectations as much as to other aspects of economic behaviour. However, it still embodied a basic behavioural irrationality: for example, even if it is as clear as daylight that a government is embarked on a spend-thrift course of high deficits and hot central bank printing presses, the theory predicted that people would not raise their expectations of inflation to realistic rates until long after the inflation has hit those rates. It defied commonsense that people should be duped in this way.

This supposition of general and lasting delusion—or fooling all the people for a long time—also ironically implies that governments can engineer long-lasting booms and reverse incipient slumps simply by turning to such inflationary (euphemistically, 'reflationary') policies. The reason is that, because expectations of inflation take off slowly, so also does inflation itself; and so the extra money pumped into the economy has a correspondingly big effect on output in the early stages, rather than being absorbed in higher prices. By the same token, governments could stop booms from getting out of hand by a timely reversal of these policies once the upswing is well assured but before inflation has taken serious hold. By such 'stabilisation' policy, governments could ameliorate, if not conquer, the business cycle, without sparking off inflation on any major scale.

Government Claims

Claims to such powers on the part of governments have lain at the heart of the Keynesian approach to policy, and have underpinned most of British post-war economic policy until 1979 and most of US economic policy from the Kennedy era until Mr Paul Volcker's inauguration as Chairman of the Fed, also in 1979.

These claims would have appeared preposterous to the old classical economists, and, who knows, perhaps also to Keynes himself in modern circumstances; they have, of course, always shocked followers of conservative economic thought. Yet these followers had for a long time no theoretical tools with which to counter this nonsense. They were confronted with 'econometric evidence' that the adaptive expectations models fitted the data and that Keynesian policies worked to maintain full employment without provoking serious inflation. The non-Keynesians either had to put up with it or shut up; they grumbled through the 1960s but basically shut up. Professor Milton Friedman, the originator and leader of the monetarist counter-revolution against Keynesian thought, had by 1970 reached a sort of truce with the Keynesians, who in turn had incorporated many of Friedman's innovations into their models. In this truce, dubbed the Neo-Classical (or Neo-Keynesian) Synthesis, monetarists and Keynesians agreed that stabilisation policies *could* work in this manner, because of the adaptiveness of expectations. Where they agreed to differ was, first, on how long it would take for the stimulatory phase of policy to produce inflation, and, second, on how beneficial stabilisation policies would be in practice. The monetarists have typically argued, first, that big inflation effects would come through within two years or so of a stimulus—more quickly than Keynesians believe. Secondly, they said governments are incapable, even if they were willing, of *timing* their interventions correctly, so that they would be as likely to *worsen* as to improve the cycle. Finally, and most damagingly, they have charged that there would in practice be an inflationary bias in government policy; governments would be happier 'stimulating' than 'deflating' the economy, and this would cause a steady upward pressure on inflation.

Hence there have been substantive and obvious differences on *policy* between monetarists and Keynesians. Nevertheless, they both subscribed to an essentially similar view (or 'model') of how the economy worked, the crucial part of which was that when policies changed people would only change their expectations *gradually* and *after* the policies had taken effect.

This intellectual truce has been shattered by the modern theory of 'Rational Expectations', which says that people use all the evidence available to them in an intelligent manner to predict inflation, profits, etc., that is, both *before* the policies take effect and afterwards. Going back to Keynes's beauty contest, speculators in the stock market are certainly worrying about what other speculators think and will think. But what Keynes missed was that they each can work out the likely outcome for the profits which underlie stock performance and they know the others can too—much as the judges know what will wash as 'beauty' in the outside world of public opinion after the contest is over. This knowledge acts as a discipline on the market; 'silly' views could in principle take hold, but everyone knows that, if they did, they would sooner or later lead to a crash *and so they will avoid them.*

The original idea was set out in 1961 by John Muth in a now famous article;[1] but it took a decade before it really caught hold of economic thinking in a major way. Pioneering work on its implications for the behaviour of the economy really started around 1970, and by the middle 1970s a lot of work was under way.

Implications for Policy

When you think about it, the theory of rational expectations is—like all good theories—obvious commonsense. But it has dramatic implications for policy. Because people intelligently

[1] J. Muth, 'Rational Expectations and the Theory of Price Movements', *Econometrica*, Vol. 29, 1961, pp. 315-35.

evaluate the likely effects of government policies, it clearly implies that government does not have the power to stabilise the economy by the methods described earlier: policies to stimulate the economy will be 'seen through' and will generate inflation rapidly. If governments are seen to be committed to some unrealistically high volume of employment in the name of 'full' employment, and to be pursuing reflationary policies with that over-riding aim, the inflation generated will rise to a point of crisis in a short time and the policies will be unsustainable. While, if carefully circumscribed, there may be some effective 'stabilisation policy', its evaluation is a highly complex matter and at the very least the chances of finding a successful formula remote, given our limited knowledge of the complex interactions between government and the behaviour of intelligently reacting people and firms. Robert Lucas (University of Chicago) and Thomas Sargent (University of Minnesota), two major pioneers in rational expectations work, have summarised it thus:

'Existing Keynesian macro-economic models cannot provide reliable guidance in the formulation of monetary, fiscal or other types of policy. This conclusion is based in part on the spectacular recent failures of these models and in part on their lack of a sound theoretical or econometric basis. . . .
'Models can be formulated which are free of these difficulties. . . . The key elements of these models are that agents are rational. . . .
'[These models] will focus attention on the need to think of policy as the choice of stable rules of the game, well understood by economic agents. . . . [They] will also suggest that policies which affect behaviour mainly because their consequences cannot be correctly diagnosed, such as monetary instability and deficit financing, have the capacity only to *disrupt*'.[2] (My italics.)

The implications go further and deeper. Suppose a government could work out such a formula for stabilising the business cycle. Why should it benefit the economy? After all, if people were already reacting intelligently to the events—perhaps adverse shocks, such as a rise in oil prices—that had hit them, they can be regarded as having already done the best that

2 R. Lucas and T. Sargent, 'After Keynesian Macro-economics', in *After the Phillips Curve: Persistence of High Inflation and High Unemployment*, Federal Reserve Bank of Boston, 1978.

could be done. Government, by smoothing out the reaction, would then be making matters *worse*. Again, it is possible to find circumstances where the economy has problems which stabilisation policies could in principle improve, but the *practical* difficulties of designing such a policy remain and the problem often has simpler cures.

The effect of generous unemployment benefits on unemployment is one such problem. In recession, these benefits will encourage more unemployment than otherwise and a lesser willingness to take wage cuts. People are acting rationally in exhibiting this unwillingness. Because the state is paying out the benefits, society as a whole is, of course, worse off if they do so. If stabilisation policy succeeded in reducing the recession, it would save society some resources. But a simpler cure for this problem would be to set benefits at lower amounts where the incentives to work are preserved reasonably intact. It would be a curious case of the tail wagging the dog if governments were to pursue vigorous stabilisation policies which risk triggering serious inflation, because they lack the courage to set benefits at realistic amounts.

Yet another implication of rational expectations is that the steady rise in unemployment we have observed over the last two decades in the Western world cannot be attributed to 'governments not spending enough'—since by the same token it could not be eliminated by a sustained government 'reflation'. It must be attributed to the economy's inefficiencies which in turn must come from ill-advised government intervention in markets—since, left to themselves, private firms and people could make a good job of the economy. This is the basis for 'supply-side' policies, broadly defined as policies to free markets from government restrictions. High tax rates ('marginal' ones—that is, the extra tax on *extra* income earned) induce people to work less; the interaction of taxes with unemployment benefits can contrive to create very high 'marginal tax rates' on the decision to work at all and induce unemployment, as well as a burgeoning of the shadow economy.

Britain is a good illustration of a country where the problem has been particularly acute. By the end of 1983 a family man with two children would have had to earn about 85 per cent of the average male manual wage to be noticeably better off

than out of work. These out-of-work benefits continue indefinitely. So in effect, if such a man decides to work, he will pay
no less than 85 per cent of his earnings back to the state, a
ridiculously high marginal tax rate! Furthermore, should his
wife decide to work when he is unemployed, she will lose no
less than 90 per cent of her extra earnings in taxes or reduced
benefits. It is not surprising that the shadow economy in
Britain is now estimated to have risen to some 16 per cent of
national income,[3] a figure which makes it seem likely that
the unemployed are involved on a major scale, since they have
a particularly large incentive to take work undeclared to the
authorities who would dock their benefits. This nexus of problems, known as the 'unemployment trap', has led to increased
emphasis in Britain on containing the rise in benefits while
urgently seeking new ways of cutting expenditure to make
room for tax cuts, especially to bring the low-paid out of the
tax net.

'Gradualism' or 'Cold Turkey' Treatment

But the problem of inflation has dominated policy discussion
since 1979. And here rational expectations has brought about
a remarkable shift of emphasis. Monetarism emphasised the
necessity—generally accepted by 1970—of reducing the growth
of the money supply to control inflation. Because of adaptive
expectations this process was seen as slow and painful even by
monetarists: if growth in the money supply were to be cut
sharply, this would mean a very bad and prolonged slump
and unemployment. They therefore advocated 'gradualism',
that is, reducing the rate of money supply growth by a few
percentage points each year, the whole process stretched out
over, say, a five- to 10-year period. In this way, the inevitable
misery of squeezing inflation out of the system would, while
admittedly stretched out over a protracted period, be prevented
from becoming a traumatic crisis.

This prescription is now under challenge. A sharp, once-for-
all cut in money supply growth ('cold turkey'), if expectations
are rational, would imply indeed a sharp shock to the economy;

[3] Kent Matthews, 'National Income and the Black Economy', *The Journal of
Economic Affairs*, Vol. 3, No. 4, July 1983, pp. 261-67.

as the régime changes there will be big errors in expectations previously formed. But new expectations would then be formed consistent with the new régime; inflation would fall rapidly, and the economy would rebound from the shock, admittedly not at once, but at a reasonable pace. By giving some warning of the régime change, it may even be possible for the government to mitigate the shock to expectations. In the electoral rhythm of democracies, 'cold turkey' started early after an election has a good chance of delivering results before the next one—the inflation results would clearly have arrived, and the recovery from the initial sharp shock would be well under way. Such, indeed, is a rough description of the policies practised both by Mrs Thatcher from the end of 1979, and by Mr Volcker at the Fed from the end of 1980. Both involved sharp contractions in monetary policy, producing rises in interest rates to unprecedentedly painful heights.

By contrast, gradualism runs the serious risk of doing little to inflation but enough to unemployment to fail to impress the electorate and so dissipate early sources of political will to reduce inflation. Its *political* feasibility is therefore in doubt as a cure for inflation. Gradualism went wrong in the USA under Nixon and Ford, in Canada between 1975 and 1981, in France under the Barre plan in the late 1970s, and in Italy under repeated attempts at moderate squeezes by the Banca d'Italia in the 1970s.

Rational Expectations and Budgetary Policy

A final aspect of counter-inflation policy must be addressed—the role of the budget deficit, a big debate in the USA today. The early classical economists never questioned the necessity of balancing the budget on average over the cycle. Keynesians, of course, discarded this belief, but one of the by-products, even under monetarism, was the downgrading of this requirement. Monetarists believe that, provided money supply growth is controlled, failure to balance the budget will affect only interest rates. A sustained budget deficit, they said, would raise interest rates and thus reduce private spending, but will not cause inflation.

Rational expectations has led to the re-instatement of the

old classical orthodoxy on budgetary policy. The monetarist belief, as far as it goes, is not questioned. The objection is that it does not go deep enough. Suppose a policy of *high* deficits and *tight* money is followed. The nation's debt will accumulate rapidly because deficits are high and, since not financed by printing money, must be financed by issuing IOUs in the only other form—government bonds or 'debt'. This *goes on* year in year out, as long as the deficits stay high (and money is not printed any faster). But clearly it *cannot* go on indefinitely. Sooner or later, *either* the nation's savers will refuse to hold any more government debt, *or* they will demand higher and higher interest rates as the price of holding more and more of it. And in this case the process will eventually be stopped by the pressures of rising interest rates. When this point comes, high deficits will continue to be possible only if money is printed faster to hold interest rates down. At this point, there will be, contrary to the dicta of the monetarists, higher inflation for sure.

If people expect inflation, inflation expectations will be high *today!* This will both give an added upward twist to interest rates and will cause the inflation to start much earlier, because people will start a 'flight from money' which itself will trigger rising prices.

So the budget deficit *does* matter because of the *political* feasibility of permanently refraining from printing money to finance it. Prudent anti-inflation policy includes containment of the deficit to an amount that can be comfortably financed at steady interest rates *without printing money*.

This has been a primary maxim of Mrs Thatcher's policies. Indeed, *more* attention has been paid to reducing the budget deficit than to the short-term movements of growth in the supply of money, because it has been felt that, provided the basic source of monetary temptation, so to speak, was bolted down, then control of money supply itself would be easier over the long term and, most importantly, market confidence in that control would be assured.

President Reagan's policies contrast with Mrs Thatcher's. The budget deficit has been allowed to rise far beyond the wildest early projections, and the consequences for money supply control have been shrugged off by the White House; Paul Volcker, Chairman of the Fed, has been left to do the best he can with it. The White House would like him *both* to control the money supply, financing the deficit by massive $50-billion per quarter bond issues, *and* keep interest rates down. From a rational expectations perspective this is possible only if there is confidence that at some future date the budget deficit will be brought down *without* printing extra money. Yet by 1985 the public sector's debt had roughly doubled in real value since the end of 1980; debt interest alone was running at over $100 billion per year. It is a tall order for the markets to believe a future American President will order a rise in taxes or cuts in spending of up to $100 billion a year to balance the books without resort to the money printing presses. The risks are obvious: a collapse of confidence in the Fed's future capacity to control the money supply (because of a political incapacity to control the deficit) would precipitate a renewed inflationary crisis in the United States—with all that that implies for the rest of us.

It is against this background that the Congressional Gramm-Rudman Amendment has acquired such significance. It proposes to eliminate the budget deficit by a series of cuts over four years; if the President and Congress fail to agree on budget details to achieve these cuts, automatic across-the-board cuts are mandated for discretionary government spending. The Supreme Court has ruled this across-the-board formula to be unconstitutional, but some alternative formula is now under discussion. From the viewpoint of market expectations, it is essential that some credible mechanism for reducing or at least controlling the budget deficit be in place.

Keynesian Counter-Attack

This revival of classical thought—appropriately termed 'new classical' economics—has provoked fierce counter-attacks from a number of directions.

One such direction has been to establish the possibility of involuntary unemployment even when people have rational expectations. In a recent work,[4] Joseph Stiglitz of Princeton University showed that, if people for some reason expect there

---

[4] J. P. Neary and J. E. Stiglitz, 'Toward a reconstruction of Keynesian economics', *Quarterly Journal of Economics*, Vol. 98, Supplement, 1983, pp. 199-228.

to be unemployment in the future, then with markets not instantaneously clearing you will get unemployment today. But the difficulty with this is to explain the reason for future unemployment when markets adjust over time. The starting point is arbitrary.

Even for this result Stiglitz requires the assumption that the labour market does not clear but has wages set for certain periods, with unemployment then varying with demand. It is well-known that, under this assumption of 'temporarily rigid' money wages, unemployment can occur in the short run and will take time to eliminate (e.g. the work of John Taylor of Stanford University[5]). This sort of unemployment is, however, hard to describe as 'involuntary' since people set these wages knowing that in some circumstances they would be unemployed; presumably it is better for them to do this than to endure the costs of fluctuating wages for the sake of continuous employment.

Other work has shown reasons why firms may wish to pay more than the 'competitive' wage (because, for example, they wish to motivate workers to stay on or because they wish to select better workers). But of course there must be something stopping the competitive wage from falling for this to produce unemployment, since otherwise the unemployed workers would keep on bidding wages down until enough employers were motivated by price to stop this behaviour. This floor beneath the competitive wage must be some government intervention such as a benefit rate—the classical analysis again.

Another direction has been concerned with the 'efficiency' of financial markets.[6] According to this theory, not only do these markets' dominant participants have rational expectations but also the prices of financial securities contain risk premia just sufficient to compensate a typical participant for the extra risk the security contributes to his diversified portfolio. One implication is that 'active' funds should not be able to make abnormal profits in the stock markets except by taking

[5] J. B. Taylor, 'Aggregate Dynamics and Staggered Contracts', *Journal of Political Economy*, Vol. 88, 1980, pp. 1-23.

[6] M. Adler and B. Dumas, 'International Portfolio Choice and Corporation Finance: A Synthesis', *Journal of Finance*, Vol. 38, No. 3, June 1983, pp. 925-995, is a most useful review of recent developments.

abnormal risks; the evidence of some systematically successful funds appears to contradict this. Another implication is that risk premia should have a stable relationship with the observable variation in security prices; some evidence particularly from the foreign exchange market casts doubt on this, though generally the evidence is favourable. Whatever the ultimate verdict on this issue, there is enough evidence to make Keynes's original idea of expectations being irrational or psychologically determined with little reference to objective realities exceptionally hard to sustain; furthermore, one may reject efficiency without rejecting rational expectations (for example, attitudes to risk may differ widely and shifts in the distribution of wealth may therefore shift the dominant group's risk premium).

In this context one should mention the views of Hyman Minsky (Washington University, St Louis) and other post-Keynesians[7] who have remained faithful to Keynes's original ideas about expectations. According to them, expectations will be dominated by waves of pessimism and optimism induced (irrationally) by the present state of business. A wave of optimism will cause a 'bubble' of credit which the wave of pessimism bursts; financial values and collateral collapse and large-scale bankruptcies precipitate a slump. While there is plenty of evidence of changes of 'sentiment' in the stock markets, this theory's prediction that they are foreseeable by a rational investor is generally rebutted; this indicates that sentiment is rational, and not a 'bubble', since a rational investor can do no better. Of course that does not mean he makes no mistakes! New information is constantly bombarding the markets, changing sentiments as people re-evaluate prospects (for dividends, defaults, etc.).

A lot of clever people have been involved in these counter-attacks; which goes to prove that the emotions are strongly stirred, presumably for political reasons, by government intervention. The evidence is by no means all favourable to the pure new classical position; but the fact that most economists now adopt rational expectations as a working assumption is testimony to the powerful impact the position has made. The

---

[7] H. Minsky, *Stabilizing an Unstable Economy*, Yale University Press, New Haven, Conn., and London, 1986; P. Davidson, *Money and the Real World*, Wiley, New York, 1972.

burden of proof has shifted noticeably onto those who wish to defend government interventions; they must now establish not merely that these will in the circumstances assumed be beneficial if carried out as planned but also that they will not be waylaid by powerful interest groups. It is usually a hard case to make.

Are Rational Expectations Unbelievable?

Some would argue that rational expectations is an unrealistic concept; that people are unlikely to use information as efficiently as the theory postulates, and that instead they use rules of thumb which are rather like 'adaptive expectations'. Others in similar vein say that, while people may indeed use information efficiently, they do not know how the economy works, and *this* uncertainty causes them to make systematic errors in their expectations; in practice, the best they can then do is again something that is rather like adaptive expectations.

Clearly, for individuals, this criticism has some force. We all know an Aunt Agatha or Uncle Fred who would be prime candidates for non-rational expectations or worse. But this objection misses the force of the argument that there are strong incentives—because people's livelihoods and firms' profits ride on them—for forecasts to be accurate; hence, when it matters, people and firms will pay professionals to produce a good forecast. These professionals will invest resources in the forecasting business because of its returns; extra business will be channelled towards the advisers who make the better forecasts. And the *best* forecasts possible are rational expectations forecasts! Thus the competitive process itself will at the least produce a strong tendency for forecasts to move towards 'full rationality'. Even if rational expectations is, strictly speaking, inaccurate as a description of expectations, it is likely to be a useful approximation, certainly more so than the assumption that people use forecasts which could easily be bettered by the application of sophisticated techniques and more information. In this respect, assuming firms have rational expectations is like assuming firms maximise profits; they may not exactly do that all the time but it is a useful approximation to complex behaviour.

Economists have rough-and-ready tools at their disposal and they have to make do with such powerful approximations. The majority in the economics profession today are taking rational expectations into their tool-kit; and they are reporting good results on the whole. Financial and commodity markets seem to behave more or less as the theory would predict; they appear to respond to new information rapidly and with well-informed assessments. Since interest rates and the exchange rate are set in such markets and play a major role in general economic behaviour, in the business cycle and inflation, at the very least rational expectations has clearly contributed this important dimension to our understanding of how the economy behaves.

But it does not stop there; in much empirical research wages have also been found to be influenced crucially by rational expectations of prices, so that the inflation process itself is now seen as driven powerfully by rational expectations of future policy. Economic research all over the world is going on at a hectic pace in these and other markets to re-examine experience in the light of the new approach; and it is steadily gaining ground. We at Liverpool University have found it to be a highly effective way of modelling and forecasting the British economy. We have had our share of mistakes but we have succeeded in predicting both the sharp slowdown in inflation that has occurred under Mrs Thatcher and the prolonged recovery now in progress. Both predictions were greeted with general incredulity by mainstream 'neo-Keynesian' forecasters when we started to make them regularly in early 1980; it was the rational expectations methods that convinced us our predictions had to be right.[8]

These methods are now being absorbed into the tool-kit of the 'mainstream forecasters'.[9] There is always a time-lag—a

---

[8] We have documented some of this experience in a recent book, *Rational Expectations and the New Macro-economics*, by Patrick Minford and David Peel, published by Martin Robertson, Oxford, 1983.

[9] Both the London Business School and the National Institute of Economic and Social Research have now adopted rational expectations in their models of the UK economy. Internationally, a recent Brookings Conference on world models revealed increasing interest in rational expectations, with three simulation models (i.e., the parameters of which were taken from previous models estimated under alternative expectations hypotheses) and one fully estimated model (the Liverpool world model) using this method.

'diffusion process'—before new methods are generally adopted in practical work. They would certainly yield dividends in forecasting the US economy and the world economy generally. As it is, by a curious irony policy-makers such as Mrs Thatcher and President Reagan have made considerable implicit use of these ideas in reinforcing and justifying their 'conservative' hunches and instincts, whereas practical economic forecasters in industry and the City of London have been rather slow to adopt them into their procedures.

The Political Implications of Rational Expectations

Let me close with a thought about *politics*, an implication of the rational expectations approach where it might be thought to be fairly irrelevant. One piece of the 'conventional wisdom' among economists has always been that to win elections politicians should depress the economy soon after a general election to squeeze inflation down in time for the next general election and then should boost the economy as this new election approaches. Inflation will still be low because it takes time to react to the boom, but incomes will be booming because of the pre-election stimulus.

According to the rational expectations approach, this is bad advice to give politicians because rational voters will see through this behaviour. They will see that inflation will revive after the election and penalise the offending politicians at the elections. It is better, or best, on the new view, for politicians to present a coherent programme, not to try clever tricks on the electorate, and to be honest about problems and tough solutions. Mrs Thatcher's re-election in 1983, when, according to the conventional political/economic wisdom, she should have been massively defeated, is a good example of this principle at work. And it had obvious relevance for President Reagan in November 1984. Pursue this thought about the rationality of voters a bit more and you will start to get optimistic about the frontiers of the 'politically possible' in economic policies in a democracy. Rational economic policies, after several decades of increasing government intervention and resulting market malfunctions, may be once again within our grasp.

7. *The General Theory,* Secular Stagnation and the World Economy

MICHAEL BEENSTOCK

Esmée Fairbairn Professor of Finance and Investment, City University Business School

Michael Beenstock

MICHAEL BEENSTOCK was born in 1946 and educated at the London School of Economics (BSc(Econ), 1967; MSc, 1968; PhD, 1976). He was Adviser, HM Treasury, 1970-76, on international monetary and energy problems; World Bank (Washington), 1976-78, on project appraisal and development planning; Senior Research Fellow, London Business School, 1978-81. Since 1981 he has been the Esmée Fairbairn Professor of Finance and Investment, City University Business School, and Director of the City Institute of Finance and Economic Review (CIFER).

He is author of *The Foreign Exchanges: Theory Modelling and Policy* (1978); *Health Migration and Development* (1980); *A Neoclassical Analysis of Macroeconomic Policy* (1980); *The World Economy in Transition* (1983); and *Insurance for Unemployment* (1986). For the IEA he has previously contributed papers, 'Fallacies in Counter-inflation Policy', to its collection of essays entitled *Could Do Better* (Occasional Paper 'Special', No. 62, 1982), and 'Social Policy for Social Democracy', to its symposium, *Agenda for Social Democracy* (Hobart Paperback 15, 1983).

The General Theory, Secular Stagnation and the World Economy

MICHAEL BEENSTOCK

Introduction: Keynes and the Theory of Secular Stagnation

To what extent does *The General Theory* suggest that Keynes supported the theory of secular stagnation? What was the relationship between *The General Theory* and Keynes's views about the structure and management of the world economy? How did he see the interdependence between these issues? Was his assessment of them correct?

Exegesis of *The General Theory* is usually difficult because, as Don Patinkin has observed,[1] ill-health, the Second World War and Keynes's relatively early death at 62 in 1946 denied him the opportunity to clarify what he really meant. Freud, Marx and Einstein, in contrast, were blessed with many years after their most important discoveries to expound, clarify and even change their minds. Thus *The General Theory* has become something of a Sphinx: it stares down at us still after 50 years, and we read into it what we will—and at our peril, because *The General Theory* is riddled with contradictions, and, as I have remarked elsewhere,[2] its over-stated style often exaggerates its case.

I do not personally understand why *The General Theory* commands so much mystique and respect. Whether or not Keynes actually said this or that in *The General Theory* or elsewhere is strictly for the Talmudists. Ideas should be judged on their own merits, whether Keynes might have uttered them or not. Pedigree does not matter; truth is everything. My guess is that, had Keynes lived as long as Freud and died in 1968 rather than 1946, much of the mystique would have faded at the grave, if he had not himself already dispelled it. This

---

[1] D. Patinkin, *Keynes' Monetary Thought: a Study of its Development*, Duke University Press, Durham, North Carolina, 1976.

[2] M. Beenstock, *A Neoclassical Analysis of Macroeconomic Policy*, Cambridge University Press, 1980, especially Ch. 2.

assessment in no way belittles Keynes's distinctive contribution to economics. Rather, it restores the supernatural to the natural.

Secular Stagnation

The theory stated

The General Theory is primarily about cyclical rather than secular economics, and its preoccupation with the short term reflected Keynes's practical interest in the here and now, rather than in the long term, 'in which we are all dead'. Nevertheless, interpreters of Keynes, such as Alvin Hansen,[3] claimed that *The General Theory* contained within it a theory of secular stagnation according to which *laissez-faire* capitalism releases recessionary forces in the long as well as in the short run.

There are two interdependent elements to this theory. In the first the marginal propensity to consume (MPC) is assumed by hypothesis to decline as society gets richer. Since the multiplier varies directly with MPC, this analysis implies that a given volume of investment spending will tend to generate less effective demand over time. In the second element, the marginal efficiency of capital (MEC) is assumed to decline as the capital stock accumulates. As profitable investment opportunities are exploited, investment tends to decline, which tends via the multiplier to depress the secular growth of effective demand. Thus secular economic growth is constrained by the satiation of consumption coupled with an inherent tendency for the volume of profitable investment opportunities to decline.

At the extreme, this logic implies that investment would become zero; effective demand and GDP would also become zero; the MPC is zero;[4] and the capital stock is very large but completely idle. It would be a curious world. Our wealth would turn out to be completely fruitless; we would have suffered the fate of Midas and starve amidst plenty.

Under classical doctrine, such a spectre of ultimate stagnation vanishes. In the classical analysis of long-run equilibrium, the rate of profit would tend towards zero, as would the rate of

---

[3] A. Hansen, *A Guide to Keynes*, McGraw-Hill, 1953.
[4] I.e., people save everything out of extra income.

savings and the rate of interest. In contrast, the rate of interest in *The General Theory* is held up by the 'liquidity trap';* whereas in the classical view of the long run both the labour force and the capital stock would be fully employed, although the economy would have stopped growing. Such is the 'Golden Age' Keynes himself dreamt of in 1930 in his 'Economic Possibilities for Our Grandchildren'.[5]

What Keynes said

I am inclined to the view that *The General Theory* is consistent with the theory of secular stagnation, but Keynes did not think it was strictly relevant to the 1930s. At some later stage, the forces of secular stagnation would become paramount unless the remedies Keynes proposed were applied. Only if investment were socialised and income redistributed from the rich to the poor (to prevent a secular decline in MPC), could he foresee how 'our grandchildren' would enjoy the golden age, and Eden be re-created. Left to itself, capitalism would fail to take us to the promised land.

The clearest statement of the theory of secular stagnation is presented in pages 217-21 of *The General Theory*, which focus on the investment aspect of the thesis, its crucial element.

'What would this involve for a society which finds itself so well equipped with capital that its marginal efficiency is zero . . .? If, in such circumstances, we start from a position of full employment, entrepreneurs will necessarily make losses if they continue to offer employment on a scale which will utilise the whole of the existing stock of capital. Hence the stock of capital and the level of employment will have to shrink until the community becomes so impoverished that the aggregate of saving has become zero . . .' (p. 217)

But on page 324 Keynes writes:

'Moreover, this situation might be reached comparatively soon—say, within twenty-five years or less . . . I assert that a state of

*Glossary, pp. 155-156.
5 Originally published in two instalments in the *Nation and Athenaeum*, 11 and 18 October 1930; subsequently reprinted in Keynes's *Essays in Persuasion*, Macmillan, London, 1931; and in D. Moggridge (ed.), *The Collected Writings of John Maynard Keynes*, Macmillan/CUP for the Royal Economic Society, Vol. IX, 1972, pp. 321-32.

full investment in the strict sense has never yet occurred, not even momentarily.'

Full investment is attained when the marginal efficiency of capital is zero. In 1936 Keynes saw this situation as a problem for the future rather than the present. On the other hand, on page 219 he claims that in Britain and the USA the process has already begun because the 'marginal efficiency has fallen more rapidly than the rate of interest . . .', causing investment to decline.

On pages 347-48, however, he seems to contradict himself:

'. . . there has been a chronic tendency throughout human history for the propensity to save to be stronger than the inducement to invest. The weakness of the inducement to invest has been at all times the key to the economic problem. Today the explanation of the weakness of this inducement may chiefly lie in the extent of existing accumulations . . .'.

This statement suggests that the secular stagnation thesis was relevant in 1936 rather than 25 years later.

It is unlikely that Keynes contradicted himself on this point, although it is well known that *The General Theory* contains numerous other contradictions. If he was contradicting himself he would have done so within only 23 pages! Most probably, he intended to say that the vortex was some way off, but that the economy was already in the whirlpool. In either case I disagree with Leijonhofvud's interpretation that Keynes's speculations '. . . referred, however, to a hypothesised and far distant future . . .' and that 'Keynes himself never advanced this not altogether respectable piece of science-fiction as a diagnosis of the 1930s'.[6] On the contrary, Keynes was a self-confessed secular stagnationist who judged those ideas to be relevant to his times as well as our own.

The second element of the theory of secular stagnation concerns the secular behaviour of the marginal propensity to consume. Keynes is in no doubt about the matter: 'These reasons will lead, as a rule, to a greater *proportion* of income being saved as real income increases' (p. 97). And as far away as on page 349, he refers to the 'growth of wealth and the

[6] A. Leijonhofvud, *On Keynesian Economics and the Economics of Keynes*, Oxford University Press, 1968, especially pp. 410-11.

diminishing marginal propensity to consume'. Finally, on page 373, he refers to the fact that the poor have higher MPCs than the rich. Keynes was therefore a believer in secular stagnation on both accounts—that is, in terms of both investment behaviour and consumption behaviour. But he considered that, in 1936, the stagnationist influences of low investment were more important than the influences of a declining MPC.

To counteract these dark forces, Keynes proposed the matter could not be left to *laissez-faire* capitalism. But nor is socialism likely to take us to the promised land (Ch. 24). Instead, he proposed a mixed-economy package consisting of the following elements:

(i)   Socialisation of investment in which the state works together with the private sector to achieve sufficient investment for the golden age to be attained (p. 378);

(ii) For the rate of interest to be kept low in order to maintain investment and to keep low the marginal propensity to save. It was for this reason that he extolled the virtues of the usury laws (Ch. 23);

(iii) For the MPC to be maintained by redistributing income from the rich to the poor (pp. 324, 373-74).

In this way the golden age could be engineered into existence and the economic possibilities for our grandchildren fully realised. It would, incidentally, lead to 'the euthanasia of the rentier class' who are 'an objectionable feature of capitalism' (pp. 221, 376). Keynes argued that capital, like land, should not have any scarcity value (p. 325).

Was Keynes right?

The secular stagnation theory is a joint hypothesis about the determinants of MPC and MEC on the one hand and the theory of liquidity preference and effective demand on the other. Within a secular framework my own empirical research suggests that interest rates and GDP are *not* determined by, respectively, the theory of liquidity preference and the theory of effective demand. Rather they are determined along the classical lines to which Keynes objected. It is for these more fundamental reasons that I am not a Keynesian secular stagnationist.

Keynesians do not have to be secular stagnationists because acceptance of the theories of effective demand and liquidity preference does not automatically imply acceptance of Keynes's secular theories of MPC and MEC. Indeed, Keynesians such as Lawrence Klein argue that:

'The long-run decline in MEC, or the American view expounded in the stagnationist thesis, is not well founded in recent developments. The cyclical and short-run aspects of Keynesian analysis can be interpreted in the light of post-war developments; the stagnation thesis seems to be less plausible.'[7]

The basic fallacy in Keynes's secular theory of MEC is that it abstracts from technical progress. Thanks to technical progress in terms of innovations in processes and products, the MEC schedule is continuously shifting to the right. What Keynes calls 'full investment' is never attained because technical progress has ensured that there is always more investment to be done. The hole is never filled in because it is always expanding. If there were no technical progress, then Keynes would surely be correct: new investment would cease as the MEC tended to zero. But where Keynes sees this tendency as a cause of deep recession the classical analysis suggests a soft landing as the golden age is approached.

Keynes was also excessively pessimistic about man's ability to consume as he became richer. Although society is much richer today than it was in 1936, there are no signs that consumers are satiated. On the contrary, man's capacity to consume appears to be endless. Thus the limits to growth are social, as Fred Hirsch claims,[8] rather than demand-constrained as claimed by Keynes. There is no iron law that implies technology must progress, or that consumption will never become satiated. But I doubt that the last 50 years have been a flash in the pan, never to be repeated. We are not running out of

[7] L. R. Klein, *The Keynesian Revolution*, Macmillan, London, second edition, 1966, p. 215.

[8] F. Hirsch, *The Social Limits to Growth*, Harvard Univerity Press, Cambridge, Mass., 1977.

projects to invest in and things on which to spend our growing incomes.

As I have argued elsewhere,[9] I give no more credence to the Keynesian stagnationists on the demand side than I do to the Kondratieff and Club-of-Rome-type stagnationists on the supply side.[10] The world is not running out of demand any more than it is running out of supply. I do not believe that stagnationist theories help us to understand why world economic growth has been lack-lustre since the 1970s. Instead, I have argued[11] that these phenomena are part of a re-structuring of the world economy as developing countries challenge the mature industrial economies, especially in the production of manufactures.

The International Economic Order

The link with Bretton Woods

Keynes's involvement in the Bretton Woods negotiations is directly linked with ideas he expressed in *The General Theory*, which, although primarily concerned with the macro-economics of a closed economy, contains a blue-print for reforming international economic relations. These proposals complement those he advanced to combat what he saw as the dark forces of secular stagnation and to help economies attain the maturity which *laissez-faire* denied them.

Keynes had long been a critic of the gold standard. Gold was a 'barbarous relic' that prevented the world from achieving an appropriate volume of effective demand and set nation against nation in competition for specie, the supply of which was haphazardly determined by nature. He applauded the abandonment of the gold standard in 1931 but feared the complete flexibility of exchange rates. He therefore welcomed the establishment of the Exchange Equalisation Account in 1932, which was designed to iron out fluctuations in the exchange rate, but objected to the secrecy of its operations.

---

[9] M. Beenstock, *The World Economy in Transition*, Allen and Unwin, London, 1983, especially Chs. 2 and 5.

[10] For example, W. W. Rostow, *The World Economy*, Macmillan, London, 1978, and D. H. Meadows *et al.*, *The Limits to Growth*, Universe, New York, 1972.

[11] M. Beenstock, *op. cit., passim.*

Indeed, in 1933 he drafted radical proposals for international monetary reform[12] which he hoped would influence the World Economic Conference of that year and which should be regarded as a precursor to his Bretton Woods proposals initiated nine years later.

In short, even before drafting *The General Theory* he had set himself against the gold standard as well as freely flexible exchange rates. He had also come out in favour of a modicum of protection but considered that the tariff war of the early 1930s was excessive and dangerous.[13] What did *The General Theory* have to say on these issues and what bearing did it have on Keynes's proposals for the shaping of the post-war economy?

The General Theory *and protectionism*

'For a favourable [trade] balance, provided it is not too large, will prove extremely stimulating; whilst an unfavourable balance may soon produce a state of persistent depression.

'It does not follow from this that the maximum degree of restriction of imports will promote the maximum favourable balance of trade. . . . There are strong presumptions of a general character against trade restrictions unless they can be justified on special grounds.' (*General Theory*, p. 338.)

According to Keynes, a favourable trade balance increases the domestic money stock, which lowers the rate of interest thereby stimulating investment. This stimulus to investment is part of the armoury required to stave off secular stagnation. Thus protection is desirable not because it protects jobs at home, but because it stimulates the quantity of money and thereby moderates the rate of interest. On the other hand, too much protection is dangerous—and for two reasons. First, it 'may lead to a senseless international competition for a favourable [trade] balance which injures all alike' (pp. 338-39). Secondly, if the trade balance is large and the rate of interest falls too far, a dramatic inflation might be triggered (p. 336) and capital will tend to flow out of the country (p. 337).

[12]*Collected Writings*, Vol. XXI, pp. 360ff.
[13]*Ibid.*, p. 236.

It seems that Keynes is saying two things, one theoretical, and the other practical. He explicitly states (p. 339) that his is a theoretical argument against free-trade doctrines. But, although he never tells us the special grounds for trade restrictions, he appears to be recommending mild protectionism as desirable both nationally and internationally. On the other hand, he says that 'great moderation is necessary, so that a country secures for itself no larger a share of the stock of the precious metals than is fair and reasonable . . .' (p. 338). This is Keynes at his most tantalising. There is after all some degree of protection that is 'fair and reasonable'; but it is never defined. But we can be certain that it did not approach the extent attained in his lifetime.

'Contemporary experience of trade restrictions in post-war Europe offers manifold examples of ill-conceived impediments on freedom which, designed to improve the favourable balance, had in fact a contrary tendency' (p. 338).

How far were Keynes's protectionist sentiments carried over into his proposals for post-war reform? It seems that, for all practical purposes, he had abandoned them altogether and become a free-trader once more.[14] But at a theoretical level there is no evidence that Keynes ever hung up his mercantilist boots for good.

The General Theory *and currencies*

'Never in history was there a method devised of such efficacy for setting each country's advantage at variance with its neighbours' as the international gold (or, formerly, silver) standard' (p. 349).

Under the gold standard, the balance of payments did not tend to self-correct, as the classical doctrine suggested. Indeed,

'Under the influence of this faulty theory the City of London gradually devised the most dangerous technique for the maintenance of equilibrium which can possibly be imagined, namely, the technique of bank rate coupled with a rigid parity of the foreign exchanges. For this meant that the objective of maintain-

[14]*Collected Writings*, Vol. XXV, p. 50.

ing a domestic rate of interest consistent with full employment was wholly ruled out' (p. 339).

Keynes therefore rejected the notion of fixed exchange rates in order to wrest monetary independence from the shackles of the gold standard.

'I am now of the opinion that the maintenance of a stable general level of money-wages is, on a balance of considerations, the most advisable policy for a closed system; whilst the same conclusion will hold good for an open system, provided that equilibrium with the rest of the world can be secured by means of fluctuating exchanges' (p. 270).

Later, on p. 340, he says that there is wisdom,

'in the last resort to restore the stock of money by devaluation, if it had become plainly deficient through an unavoidable foreign drain, a rise in the wage unit, or any other cause'.

Page 270 suggests flexible exchange rates. Page 340 suggests adjustable exchange rates. I suspect that Keynes never really intended flexible rates, for two reasons. First, it would be inconsistent with his argument in Chapter 12 that investors are irrational in the way they form expectations. For Keynes, speculators are anti-social 'South Sea bubble-makers' who generate false asset prices that have little or nothing to do with the fundamentals. Keynes gives short shrift to what economists today call rational expectations. Although he relates his discussion to the behaviour of share prices, it is unlikely that he thought differently about speculative influences upon floating exchange rates. Just as on page 164 he suggests that the state is likely to have a more sensible view about the proper marginal efficiency of capital, so we can equally infer that the state is likely to have a more sensible view about what the exchange rate should be.

I have noted elsewhere[15] that Keynes's criticisms are contradicted by the empirical evidence in favour of market efficiency and that they may even have been personally motivated. For Keynes, who saw himself as having rational expectations, and who was a gambler in his earlier years, came near to bankruptcy in at least two bear markets, one of which involved

[15] In my *A Neoclassical Analysis of Macroeconomic Policy, op. cit.*, Ch. 2.

currency speculation. No doubt it was partly for this reason that Keynes was a staunch supporter of permanent exchange controls.[16] He wished to remove the speculative element from international investment and exchange-rate determination as part of his proposals for the post-war international economic order. The second reason why I do not believe that Keynes intended flexible exchange rates is that these proposals explicitly ruled them out. He suggested that floating exchange rates are likely to be unstable and that fixed but adjustable exchange rates should be operated.[17] This view, of course, became the basic doctrine at Bretton Woods.

In short, *The General Theory* rejected the gold standard in favour of a system of adjustable exchange rates rather than freely floating exchange rates. Both in terms of stock market and currency behaviour, the balance of academic research is weighted in favour of the hypothesis that markets are efficient in using information, thus suggesting that Keynes's views were incorrect. Currency and stock markets might be volatile, but not because of the reasons Keynes gave. Nor does it follow that inhibiting the flexibility of exchange rates, as he suggests, is desirable, any more than it would be appropriate for the Bank of England to intervene in the stock market. It is arguable that the rational expectations approach which Keynes rejected has proved more empirically useful than its early critics, Keynes included, anticipated.

Commodity markets

At the end of the war, Keynes sought the establishment of buffer stocks for the major primary commodities, although without success. The buffer-stock authorities would counter-balance de-stabilising speculation and smooth out price fluctuations.[18] Subsequent theoretical work on the economics of profitable speculation undermines much of Keynes's thesis that speculation will be de-stabilising. Page 160 of *The General Theory* refers specifically to the unstable character of commodity

[16]*Collected Writings*, Vol. XXV, pp. 31, 52 and 187.
[17]*Ibid.*, pp. 22-3, 34 and 108.
[18]*Collected Writings*, Vol. XXVII, Ch. 3.

markets, which Keynes brackets together with stock markets, and his proposals for the post-war international economic order should be related to this theme.

Keynes objected to commodity agreements in which production quotas are set. He would not have favoured present-day arrangements for coffee, and presumably he would have favoured the recent operations of the International Tin Council, though not the outcome.[19] He favoured the stabilisation of commodity prices because he thought it would inhibit the international transmission of boom and slump. A world slump tends to feed off itself if it unduly depresses commodity prices, so that primary producing countries subsequently have to lower their imports.

But this argument is all part and parcel of an underlying theme in *The General Theory*: that the market is inefficient, that *laissez-faire* does not work, and that the state must come to the rescue. Moreover, left to itself *laissez-faire* would destroy capitalism and run the risk of replacement by communism.

'It is certain that the world will not much longer tolerate the unemployment which, apart from brief intervals of excitement, is associated—and, in my opinion, inevitably associated—with present-day capitalistic individualism' (p. 381).

Keynesianism would help capitalism save itself from itself through the counsel of wise men. This claim applied as much to commodity prices as it did to currency prices, interest rates and investment. His opinions about domestic and international economic arrangements were entirely complementary.

Contemporary Relevance

In summary, Keynes in *The General Theory* was a secular stagnationist who saw 'Keynesianism' as a technique to help capitalism achieve its full potential so that our grandchildren's golden economic possibilities could be safely realised. To promote this maturity, an international economic order was required which resembled what eventually became the Bretton Woods system, that is, an arrangement which would provide

[19]It collapsed in 1986.

the necessary degree of stability in trade, currency movements and commodity prices.

As already noted, even distinguished Keynesians have abandoned his secular stagnation thesis and the 'doomwatchers' who look forward to decades of economic decline do not, by and large, base their thinking on the Keynesian analysis of secular stagnation. Instead, they speak of various supply-side constraints—depletion of natural resources, the role of pressure groups in mature economies, the changing balance of comparative advantage, and the like. They also speak of 'technological unemployment' and the coming of the 'Third Industrial Revolution', based on micro-electronics, as a cause of secular imbalance and decline. These claims are far removed from Keynes's fear that entrepreneurs would run out of profitable projects in which to invest.

We can safely say that his stagnation thesis has even less relevance today than it did 50 years ago. Personally, I would argue that historicist notions of secular stagnation, Keynesian or otherwise, do not contribute to our understanding of economic development. There are no iron laws of economic development of either a pessimistic or optimistic variety. Everything lies in the hands of man, everything is subject to change, whether for good or evil. The intellectual obsession with trends in secular economic behaviour and human behaviour more generally stretches from Alvin Toffler today through Marx and Keynes as far back as Herodotus. In Keynes's case I suspect that his paternalistic and élitist education, with its emphasis on service to the community, encouraged him to discover a deep-seated problem that could be administered away by an appropriate coterie of well-intentioned and wise men. I also suspect that this meddlesome mentality continues to run deep among the British educated establishment.

Of more practical relevance are Keynes's views about how the world economy should be organised. The Bretton Woods system (which fell considerably short of what Keynes sought) collapsed in 1971, some 15 years ago. Despite some early Gaullist attempts to resuscitate the gold standard, the world opted for floating exchange rates. At present there is much soul-searching whether these arrangements should continue or whether we should revert to some form of administered exchange rates. It is argued that real exchange rates are too volatile and that pegging the exchange rate would reduce this volatility. This response is superficial, and the cure, such as it is, is cosmetic rather than substantive. The fundamental issue is why wages and prices do not adjust themselves as fluidly as exchange rates. The rigidity of wages and prices is a basic premise in *The General Theory*. And so we have come full circle. It seems to me that the cure is not to interfere with the foreign exchange markets but to liberalise the labour and product markets so that wages and prices become as flexible as exchange rates.

In *The General Theory* Keynes addressed wage rigidity in both positive and normative terms. At times he treats it as a constraint; at other times he regards it as a desirable feature of economic behaviour. The majority of economists today would welcome with open arms a cure for wage inflexibility, and the Keynesian counter-revolutionaries have long since pointed out that wage-price flexibility completely undermines the Keynesian paradigm. In these respects I think there is more practical relevance in Pigou's *Theory of Unemployment*, which was rebuked in *The General Theory*, than there is in *The General Theory* itself. The root causes of wage rigidity should be tackled head on; *The General Theory* has done us the disservice of distracting our attention from this basic social problem by proposing all manner of second- and third-best solutions to accommodate it.

As a practical free-trader, Keynes is more relevant today than he was 50 years ago, and it is sad to see so many Keynesians arguing for protectionism. Indeed, this aspect of the Bretton Woods system (via GATT) is perhaps the only one that is worth preserving. In any case, Keynes never argued in *The General Theory* for protectionism, on the familiar grounds that this policy would directly protect jobs, as already noted.

Finally, his proposals for the stabilisation of international commodity prices (referred to earlier) were not accepted at the time, but they have subsequently been an important element in proposals for reform of the international economic order (*cf.* the Brandt Commission), and a number of commodity agreements have been in operation with various degrees of success at various times. If Keynes was correct, buffer-stock authorities should have been able to stay in profit. That they have not (the International Tin Council is the most obvious example) suggests that his ideas were too optimistic.

Coda

The world celebrated the 25th anniversary of *The General Theory* with acclaim even from the sceptics, such as the late Harry G. Johnson.[20] Fifty years on, the Sphinx seems increasingly irrelevant. One hundred years on I expect it will be lost in the oblivion of history.

---

[20]E.g., 'The General Theory after Twenty-five Years', in *Money, Trade and Economic Growth*, George Allen and Unwin, London, 1962.

8. On Keynesian Unemployment and the Unemployment of Keynes

ALAN BUDD

Professor of Economics,
London Business School

Alan Budd

ALAN BUDD has been Williams and Glyn's Research Fellow in Banking, London Graduate School of Business Studies, since 1974; now Professor of Economics. Universities of Southampton, 1966-69, and Carnegie-Mellon, 1969-70. Senior Economic Adviser, Treasury, 1970-74. Editor, *Economic Outlook*; author of *The Politics of Economic Planning* (1978). For the IEA, he contributed a paper, 'Disarming the Treasury', to the Seminar, *The Taming of Government* (IEA Readings No. 21, 1979).

On Keynesian Unemployment
and the Unemployment of Keynes

ALAN BUDD

Perhaps we should start by deciding whether we are trying to understand unemployment or trying to understand Keynes. I am primarily concerned with trying to understand unemployment, but in a volume dedicated to Keynes we must ask how far his ideas are relevant to today's events. It would be surprising if everything that Keynes had to say about unemployment were still believed to be correct, and it would be even more surprising if he had said things which would help to explain unemployment but which have been overlooked by later commentators. I cannot therefore offer any amazing revelations.

I start by recalling some of the things that Keynes said about unemployment in the inter-war period, first in his polemical writing and then in his more scholarly works. I then consider, briefly, some of the subsequent controversies about his theories and the developments in the theory of unemployment. Finally, I consider how far his work, particularly as presented in the *General Theory*, can explain unemployment today.

I conclude that Keynes's challenge to orthodox thinking remains valid but that does not mean, unfortunately, that we can simply apply Keynesian solutions to today's problems.

'Can Lloyd George Do It?'

A good example of Keynes's polemical writing on unemployment is provided by *Can Lloyd George Do It?*, a pamphlet written jointly with Hubert Henderson in support of Lloyd George's 1929 General Election pledge to cut unemployment by a programme of public spending. By 1929, apart from a brief recovery in 1924, unemployment had been more than 10 per cent for more than 10 years—'a fact unprecedented in our history', as the authors described it. Keynes catalogued the costs, in dole payments and in lost output, of prolonged high unemployment. The Liberal programme called for expenditure

139

of £100 million a year and Keynes argued that this was modest both in absolute terms and by comparison with the costs of unemployment.

'Nothing has been included in the programme which cannot be justified as worth doing for its own sake. Yet even if half of it were to be wasted, *we should still be better off.* Was there ever a stronger case for a little boldness, for taking a risk if there be one?

'It may seem very wise to sit back and wag the head. But while we wait, the unused labour of the workless is not piling up to our credit in a bank, ready to be used at some later date. It is running irrevocably to waste; it is irretrievably lost. Every puff of Mr Baldwin's pipe costs us thousands of pounds.'[1]

In *Can Lloyd George Do It?* Keynes was not primarily concerned with the causes of unemployment. However, he clearly believed that the solution lay in the expansion of demand. He directed his scorn at those who doubted that it would work:

'The Conservative belief that there is some law of nature which prevents them from being employed, that it is "rash" to employ men, and that it is financially "sound" to maintain a tenth of the population in idleness for an indefinite period, is crazily improbable—the sort of thing which no man could believe who had not had his head fuddled with nonsense for years and years.'[2]

Keynes rejected the Treasury orthodoxy that any money raised by the state to finance capital spending must diminish pound for pound the supply of funds available for industry. He also rejected the idea that increased capital spending would cause inflation:

'The suggestion that a policy of capital expenditure, if it does not take capital away from ordinary industry, will spell inflation, would be true enough if we were dealing with boom conditions. And it would become true if the policy of capital expenditure were pushed unduly fast, so that the demand for savings began to exceed the supply. But we are far, indeed, from such a position at the present time . . . To bring up the bogy of inflation as an objection to capital expenditure at the present time is like warning a patient who is wasting away from emaciation of the dangers of excessive corpulence'.[3]

[1] Keynes [1929], p. 93.   [2] *Ibid.*, p. 90.   [3] *Ibid.*, p. 117.

Splendid stuff! And Keynes's claim that his views were supported by all reasonable people brings to mind the more recent letter of the 364 economists:

> 'Indeed, we have not been able to discover any recent pronouncements to the contrary, outside the ranks of the Treasury, by an economist of weight or reputation.'[4]

Keynes argued that the cause of unemployment was inadequate demand, 'the general failure of industry as a whole to show absorbtive power'. He expanded these ideas further in 'The Great Slump of 1930' and in other essays in the early 1930s, but it was in *The General Theory* that he set out his ideas most fully.

Unemployment and The General Theory

There can be nothing new to be said about *The General Theory*. Keynes's arguments about unemployment can be summarised as follows:

(i)   There are three types of unemployment—'frictional', 'voluntary' and 'involuntary'.

(ii) 'Frictional' and 'voluntary' unemployment are the types familiar to classical economists.

(iii) 'Involuntary' unemployment is such that the unemployed would be prepared to work at below the current real wage.

(iv) 'Involuntary' unemployment is due to inadequate aggregate demand.

(v)   Wage flexibility does not cure involuntary unemployment.

Each element of that summary can be expanded briefly. Keynes distinguished between two types of classical unemployment. The first type was frictional unemployment, which allows for

> 'various inexactnesses of adjustment which stand in the way of continuous full employment: for example, unemployment due

---

4 *Ibid.*, p. 121.

to a temporary want of balance between the relative quantities of specialised resources as a result of miscalculation or inter-mittent demand; or to time-lags consequent on unforeseen changes; or to the fact that the change-over from one employment to another cannot be effected without a certain delay, so that there will always exist in non-static society a proportion of resources unemployed "between jobs".'[5]

The second type of classical unemployment which Keynes called 'voluntary' was

'due to the refusal or inability of a unit of labour, as a result of legislation or social practices or of combination for collective bargaining or of slow response to change or of mere human obstinacy, to accept a reward corresponding to the value of the product attributable to its marginal productivity'.[6]

We can use Keynes's own definition of involuntary unemployment:

'Men are involuntarily unemployed if, in the event of a small rise in the price of wage-goods relatively to the money-wage, both the aggregate supply of labour willing to work for the current money-wage and the aggregate demand for it at that wage would be greater than the existing volume of employment.'[7]

Having defined involuntary unemployment in Chapter 2, Keynes did not return to it until Chapter 19 because he spent the intervening chapters developing his theory of aggregate demand in order to show how involuntary unemployment could arise and persist.

It is important, if we are to judge Keynes's relevance to the current debate, to ask what part was played by wages, both money and real, in setting the level of unemployment. Keynes gave part of the answer in the early part of *The General Theory* (Chapter 2) but developed it more fully in Chapter 19. The main elements of his argument are as follows:

(i)   Cuts in money wages are generally resisted.

(ii) Even if they take place they do not necessarily generate changes in real wages. (They may even be associated with *rises* in real wages, if prices fall faster.)

[5] Keynes [1936], p. 6.   [6] *Ibid.*, p. 6.   [7] *Ibid.*, p. 15.

(iii) Changes in real wages do not cause changes in output and employment. If anything, the causation runs in the opposite direction. Changes in output (induced by changes in aggregate demand) cause changes in employment and real wages.

In *The General Theory* Keynes stated quite clearly that an increase in employment required a fall in real wages. He accepted the first classical postulate and implied, thereby, that firms hired labour to the point at which its marginal product was equal to the real wage. On the assumption that they faced a downward-sloping marginal productivity curve, firms would only hire more workers if real wages fell. Thus an increase in employment required both an increase in aggregate demand *and* a fall in real wages.

It is historically inaccurate to describe as 'Keynesian' unemployment that can be reduced without a fall in real wages. However, it is by now, presumably, too late to do anything about it. A better classification might be as follows:

(i) 'Keynesian' unemployment which can be reduced simply by expanding aggregate demand.

(ii) 'General Theory' unemployment which can be reduced by an increase in aggregate demand and a consequent fall in real wages.

(iii) 'Classical' unemployment which cannot be reduced by an increase in aggregate demand.

It is said that Keynes later changed his mind about the necessity for a fall in real wages and one can imagine that the general approach of *The General Theory* would allow him to do so. However, we cannot possibly draw from *The General Theory* any support for the view that flexible wages alone will cut unemployment.

'To suppose that a flexible wage policy is a right and proper adjunct of a system which on the whole is one of *laissez-faire*, is the opposite of the truth.'[8]

Wage cuts could increase employment only if aggregate demand increased. Even in a closed economy there was no

[8] *Ibid.*, p. 269.

general reason to suppose that wage cuts alone would do the trick. Keynes admitted that it might be true in an open economy but that would simply shift the problem of unemployment from one economy to another.

Fifty years after the publication of *The General Theory*, recorded unemployment is above 13 per cent, with a substantial proportion of long-term unemployed.[9] Unemployment has been above 10 per cent since 1981 and male unemployment is over 15 per cent. At the same time we have a government which resists calls for reflation of demand and relies instead on microeconomic policy.[10] It would appear that Keynes's views have been rejected. In relation to *The General Theory* the rejection must be based on the view either that Keynes's theories were wrong or that current unemployment is voluntary. I consider these possibilities in the following sections.

Macro-economics after Keynes

The Keynes industry has been hard at work for the past 50 years. One line of controversy has concerned Keynes's assertion that there can be equilibrium with involuntary unemployment. Elements of the debate can be found in Patinkin [1976], Clower [1965], Leijonhufvud [1968], Malinvaud [1977], Johnson [1961] and Meltzer [1981]. Some of the debate, one suspects, would have received little sympathy from Keynes. For example, one might imagine the following conversation about the role of flexible money wages:

Clever post-Keynesian analyst (CPKA): 'Do you realise that you only have prolonged unemployment in *The General Theory* because money wages are inflexible?'

Keynes (K): 'That cannot be. I argue that, as a matter of fact, workers tend to resist wage cuts but I specifically state that that is not fundamental to my analysis. I argue that even if money

---

[9] It is a matter of controversy how far the figure of 13 per cent reflects genuine unemployment. The Labour Force Survey of 1985 shows that nearly 900,000 who were on the register and in receipt of benefit were not seeking work during the week of the survey.

[10] The Government's views are fully described in Nigel Lawson's Mais Lecture, 'The British Experiment', 18 June 1984.

wages were flexible this would not help. There is no necessary connection between changes in money wages and changes in real wages. We cannot even be sure that they have the same sign.'

CPKA: 'But if money wages were flexible, we should see an expansion of demand for labour in response to a fall in money wages relative to prices.'

K: 'You have assumed away the problem I was emphasising. A cut in money wages will only be associated with a fall in real wages if there are other mechanisms which expand aggregate demand. A cut in money wages cannot by itself cause a rise in aggregate demand. What is needed is a rise in investment but this fails to happen because interest rates cannot fall sufficiently.'

CPKA: 'You have forgotten the Pigou effect.* Eventually prices (and wages) will fall sufficiently to raise the real value of money balances created by government and aggregate demand will expand to restore full employment.'

K: 'I discuss this point in Chapter 19. I argue that increases in real money balances either have little effect on investment (if the changes are small) or have totally unpredictable effects (if the changes are large). My actual words are "so a moderate reduction in money-wages may prove inadequate, whilst an immoderate reduction might shatter confidence even if it were practicable".'

The debate continues. We may now place rather less emphasis on the role of investment in maintaining aggregate demand. We may also believe that we know rather more about the possible obstacles to full-employment equilibrium. There is no consensus, but we might be able to get 90 per cent of economists to agree that flexible wages will not *necessarily* ensure full employment. To that extent Keynes's views have been modified. (The other 10 per cent will include those who believe that flexible wages are irrelevant and those who believe that they are sufficient to achieve full employment. The 90

*Glossary, p. 158.

per cent, of course, are not necessarily right.) But it is important to emphasise, as Meltzer does, that Keynes believed that the main bar to full employment lay not with the operation of the labour market but with the operation of the market for fixed capital.

Post-Keynesian economics has not simply consisted of attempts to destroy or enhance Keynes's reputation as an economic theorist. In relation to unemployment we have had the rise and fall (and partial rehabilitation) of the Phillips curve, though that was not, in its original form, a theory of unemployment. We have had the natural rate of unemployment and its close cousin (or identical twin) the non-accelerating inflation rate of unemployment. For those who are prepared to use the concept of the natural rate (or the NAIRU), we have had controversies, for example, between Minford [1983] and Nickell [1983] about what has caused it to change. We have had the theory of implicit contracts to explain why wages might be inflexible in the short term. We have had bargaining theories of wages to explain the setting of wages in the unionised sector. More recently we have had the theory of 'insiders' and 'outsiders' as a further possible explanation for the combination of high unemployment with continued rises in real wages for those who are employed. Finally, we have had 'hysteresis'[11] which seeks to explain why the natural rate of unemployment might respond to the past history of unemployment. In particular, it argues that a period of prolonged high unemployment raises the natural rate.

What Survives of The General Theory?

We might not necessarily accept Keynes's explanation why there can be persistent involuntary unemployment, but alternative theories can be found, in the Keynesian tradition, which produce the same result. Whether persistent involuntary unemployment is a condition of full general equilibrium or is simply an accompaniment of a prolonged—possibly infinitely prolonged—disequilibrium does not really concern us. (We all know what Keynes said about the long run.) The distinction

[11]The 'hysteresis' hypothesis suggests that future employability depends on the duration of unemployment.

between voluntary and involuntary unemployment remains, I believe, crucial. Keynes argued that an expansion of aggregate demand was both necessary and sufficient to cut involuntary unemployment. (The fall in real wages was an inevitable accompaniment of an expansion of demand through its effect in raising prices.)

The cures for voluntary unemployment include improvements in organisation or foresight which reduce frictional unemployment, a decrease in the marginal disutility of labour (a move which we would now identify as a shift in the supply curve of labour), and increases in labour productivity. One relevant point is that if those who are voluntarily unemployed (on Keynes's definition) decides to offer their labour at a lower wage, they do not thereby become employed, but merely join the ranks of the involuntary unemployed.

If we wish to consider today's problems and if we believe that Keynes's analysis is still useful, we have to decide whether unemployment is voluntary or involuntary. But we also have to consider a possibility, unfamiliar to Keynes, that increases in demand cannot even cure involuntary unemployment.

Keynes and Unemployment Today

What would Keynes say now? He would be puzzled, at least briefly, by the conjunction of unemployment and inflation. In *The General Theory*, inflation only occurs as full employment is approached. Thus it would seem that inflation must imply that all unemployment is frictional or voluntary. I suspect, however, that Keynes would soon accept that there can simultaneously be inflation and involuntary unemployment, with pay settlements more than taking account of expected price changes.

If there is involuntary unemployment, it might appear that it is easier to achieve a fall in real wages since all that is needed is for money wages to rise less rapidly than prices. That is much easier than engineering a fall in money wages while prices are unchanged. However, in the spirit of *The General Theory* Keynes could argue that even under conditions of inflation workers cannot by their own actions generate a cut in real wages. Real wages can fall only if aggregate demand rises and firms move down their demand curve for labour (the marginal productivity of labour curve). If there is involuntary unemployment, the solution is to expand aggregate demand. There will be a temporary acceleration of price inflation relative to wage inflation which will cut real wages once and for all. The result will be a fall in unemployment. But it is the expansion of demand, not the fall in real wages, which is the essential step. If we have involuntary unemployment, the only solution, in the Keynesian tradition, is to expand aggregate demand. Keynes would do this by encouraging investment, not (except possibly in the short term) by increasing the size of the budget deficit.

At the risk of over-simplification, we can now identify three approaches to unemployment. Two are descended from Keynes, the third reverts to the pre-Keynesian tradition. The first approach identifies unemployment (unhistorically) as 'Keynesian'. It argues that unemployment can be cut without any need for a fall in real wages. This view may be based on the idea that marginal costs are constant or it may imply that goods markets have not cleared. In either event, firms are prepared to expand supply (in response to a rise in demand) without requiring a rise in prices relative to wages. Since no fall in real wages is required, the solution does not require an acceleration of inflation under current conditions. Thus there is a 'free lunch'.[12] The lunch is not, however, quite so free if we recognise that the government actually wants to achieve a further fall in inflation.

The General Theory approach recognises that an expansion of demand must be accompanied by a fall in real wages. Keynes assumed that the fall in real wages will not be resisted (indeed, that is implicit in his definition of involuntary unemployment). However, modern Keynesians might not be so sure. Despite the existence of involuntary unemployment, labour markets might so operate that cuts in real wages were vigorously resisted by those in work. Thus we have Professor Layard and Professor Meade, with their rather different schemes, arguing that a Keynesian expansion of demand must be accompanied by incomes policies.[13]

[12]Layard *et al.* [1984].

[13]E.g., J. E. Meade, *Wage-Fixing Revisited*, Occasional Paper 72, IEA, 1985.

Finally, we have the classical approach. In its most extreme form it assumes that labour markets clear instantly and that all unemployment is voluntary. That does not necessarily mean that unemployment is not a problem, but if it is a problem the solution must lie in changing the constraints which bring about the current equilibrium. Hence the proposals for cuts in social security payments, further changes in trade union law, abolition of wages councils, etc. Less extreme forms of the classical approach recognise that the labour market has not cleared and seek ways to speed up the process, though adherents to the classical approach do not generally accept that an expansion of demand (even temporarily) can be used.

'Thatcherism' and Unemployment

Mrs Thatcher's Conservative Government does not consistently rely on any one of the three approaches and that is no doubt wise. It was Mr Callaghan in 1976 who famously pronounced the end of the Keynesian approach to employment policy and the present Government has continued to reject calls for expansion of demand. But it is not consistently classical in its approach. For example, it is willing to welcome projects such as the Channel Tunnel on the ground that they 'create jobs' whereas a classical economist would see jobs as a cost rather than a benefit. It has also, somewhat inconsistently, explained recession and accompanying increases in unemployment in Britain by reference to world economic developments. If external changes in demand can affect employment, so can internal ones.

The present UK government also tries to cure unemployment by 'talking down' wages, which brings it into disfavour with all sides. The Keynesians object because wage moderation on its own will do no good and may even make matters worse. Classical economists object because the government should mind its own business. If it does not like people's rational behaviour it should change the constraints. It may be said here that the Government appears to be rather closer to the Keynesians since it promises—through its target for money GDP—to maintain a given growth of nominal demand. In his 1985 Budget speech Mr Lawson said:

'A policy for demand expressed unambiguously in terms of money provides a further important advantage. For it ensures that wage restraint *will* provide more jobs. I repeat to-day the undertaking I gave the National Economic Development Council last month: the Medium-Term Financial Strategy is as firm a guarantee against inadequate money demand as it is against excessive monetary demand.'

While the Chancellor's statement appears to recognise the possibility that lower real wages might at first reduce aggregate demand, it is clear that demand management is secondary to the role of wage adjustment. Wage adjustment must lead; the maintenance of nominal demand will, if necessary, follow.

It would be pleasant to produce, at this late stage, a hitherto unnoticed footnote of Keynes which would reconcile the differences between the approaches and lead us forward to a solution. Alas, it is not to be. Keynes was convinced that wage flexibility could not restore full employment. The subsequent debate has not resolved the issue. If we have involuntary unemployment, in Keynes's sense, and if there is an intractable problem (over any reasonable time horizon) of aggregate demand, then 'supply-side' measures by themselves will help little. The only role of such measures is to lower the natural rate or NAIRU; the essential requirement is an expansion of demand. According to the classical approach, only supply-side measures will work; attempts to expand demand will simply cause inflation.

The Keynesians have had to recognise that it was the mindless application of 'Keynesian' policies which brought us to our present pass. Squeezing inflation out of the system has been an extremely painful process and we cannot be sure that it has yet been achieved. No one could possibly claim Keynes's support for the view that inflation does not matter. In *The General Theory* he decided that, on balance, rising wages and stable prices were better, in the long run, than stable wages and falling prices, but he would not have countenanced inflation. We have also learned in recent years that it was wrong to concentrate on demand conditions to the complete exclusion of supply-side conditions, but that does not necessarily mean that we need only consider the supply side.

Is There a Compromise Approach to Employment Policy?

It is not easy to suggest a compromise. Keynes believed that markets could be left to operate freely except in the case of investment:

> 'I conceive, therefore, that a somewhat comprehensive social-isation of investment will prove the only means of securing an approximation to full employment; though this need not exclude all manner of compromises and of devices by which public authority will co-operate with private initiative.'[14]

That suggests that those who call for a larger state role in investment are inheritors of the Keynesian tradition. It also appears that others in the Keynesian tradition believe that incomes policies must be added to demand management. We seem to be moving rather a long way from markets even if the design of the policies tries to incorporate their benefits.

It is difficult to argue that the present scale of unemployment is acceptable. If it is 'voluntary', it is hard to believe that we really want a system under which 13 per cent of the labour force apparently chooses leisure at the expense of the rest of the workforce. If it is involuntary, there is clearly something wrong. As far as solutions are concerned we are asked to choose between those, in the Keynesian tradition, which expand demand while offering wage restraint if necessary, and those closer to the classical tradition which encourage voluntary wage restraint while offering the maintenance of nominal demand if necessary. Both sides are ready, though with differing enthusiasm, to apply second-best solutions to particularly intractable problems of unemployment in terms of duration or location.

One particular dilemma, for those who support the application of free-market mechanisms, is as follows. There is empirical evidence to suggest that, contrary to *The General Theory*, wage moderation will cause a rise in employment. This is supported, for example, by the current version of the London Business School model, and it does not simply rely on favourable trade effects. Also, in the UK, there appears to be a well-established dynamic version of the Pigou effect in which the

[14]Keynes [1936], p. 378.

personal sector's savings ratio falls when inflation falls. Thus wage moderation is an answer to unemployment. But wage settlements seem to be unresponsive to the level of unemployment. Thus we might have to wait a long time for the beneficial effects of market forces to become apparent. But does that mean we should accept incomes policies? It is very difficult; but if there were simple solutions to these problems we would have discovered them long ago.

REFERENCES

Clower, R. [1965]: 'The Keynesian Counterrevolution: A Theoretical Appraisal', in F. H. Hahn and F. P. R. Brechling (eds.), *Theory of Interest Rates: Proceedings of a Conference held by the International Economics Association*, London: Macmillan.

Johnson, H. G. [1961]: 'The *General Theory* after Twenty-Five Years', *American Economic Review*, May.

Keynes, J. M. [1929]: 'Can Lloyd George Do It?', *Collected Writings*, Vol. IX.

Keynes, J. M. [1930]: 'The Great Slump', *Collected Writings*, Vol. IX.

Keynes, J. M. [1936]: *The General Theory of Employment, Interest and Money*, London: Macmillan.

Layard, R., G. Basevi, O. Blanchard, W. Buiter and R. Dornbusch [1984]: 'Europe: the case for unsustainable growth', *Centre for European Policy Studies*, Paper No. 8/9.

Leijonhufvud, A. [1968]: *On Keynesian Economics and the Economics of Keynes*, New York: OUP.

Malinvaud, E. [1977]: *The Theory of Unemployment Reconsidered*, Oxford: Blackwell.

Meltzer, A. [1982]: 'Keynes's *General Theory*: A Different Perspective', *Journal of Economic Literature*, March.

Minford, P. [1983]: *Unemployment: Cause and Cure*, Oxford: Martin Robertson.

Nickell, S. J. [1983]: 'A Review of *Unemployment: Cause and Cure*', *Economic Journal*, December.

Glossary

AUSTRIAN ECONOMICS: The Austrian school of economics emerged in the late 19th century, and is distinguished from other schools by its emphasis upon the subjective nature of value and costs. Contemporary neo-Austrian economists are noted for their attention to the market process of competition and to the co-ordinating role of the price system at the microeconomic level, rather than to market equilibrium.

AVERAGE PROPENSITY TO CONSUME (APC): The ratio of aggregate consumer spending to national income.

AVERAGE PROPENSITY TO SAVE (APS): The ratio of aggregate savings to national income. Also known as the 'savings ratio'.

BRETTON WOODS SYSTEM: A system of fixed exchange rates (ultimately fixed in relation to the US dollar and to gold), maintained by central banks buying and selling currencies, established by agreement between 44 countries at a conference in Bretton Woods, New Hampshire, in 1944 (and put into operation in 1945) in which Keynes played a leading part. The Bretton Woods system collapsed in the early 1970s, to be replaced by floating exchange rates between major currencies, now modified by the fixed-rate European Monetary System covering most EEC currencies, though not sterling, and by 'alignment' agreements on the US dollar, the Japanese yen, and the Swiss franc.

CLASSICAL ECONOMICS/DOCTRINE: Marx used this phrase to describe the school of thought of David Ricardo and his *predecessors*, such as Adam Smith. Keynes in the *General Theory* used the term to cover also the neo-classical successors of Ricardo, such as Marshall and Pigou. Some would even use the term (as with Budd, in this collection) to include contemporary exponents of market analysis.

153

CONSUMPTION FUNCTION: The relationship between aggregate consumer spending and its presumed determinants. *The General Theory* accepted that there were many such determinants, but fastened upon one as the prime determinant: current (disposable) national income. This relationship was assumed to be of a particular form, with both the MPC and APC declining as current national income rose. Friedman and others have disputed that *current* income is the prime variable determining consumption.

DISEQUILIBRIUM PROCESS: What happens in a market when demand and supply are not in balance.

EFFECTIVE DEMAND: The aggregate income which employers of all kinds expect to receive from the totality of their production and sales decisions. In Keynesian theory, effective demand may be less than the aggregate demand necessary to maintain full employment for long periods, unless bolstered by government spending or direction of investment.

FINE-TUNING: The Keynesian policy notion that the economy may be kept upon a stable growth path of output and full employment by continuous and appropriate variations in monetary, fiscal, and foreign exchange-rate policies.

FISCAL POLICY MULTIPLIERS: ratios measuring the estimated change in real national income arising from either an increase in government spending, or a cut in the general level of taxation, or a boost to the budget deficit, or a 'balanced expansion' of government spending and taxation of equal magnitude (the latter being called the 'balanced budget multiplier').

GOLD STANDARD: A monetary system under which the value of a currency issued by the state is fixed by law in terms of a certain quantity of gold per unit of currency, and which the monetary authorities are formally required to pay upon demand to those presenting currency to them. Under a gold standard, exchange rates between currencies are fixed within limits determined by the cost of transporting gold between countries. Most major trading countries abandoned the gold standard in 1931, but the collapse of the Bretton Woods system in the 1970s, and continued fears of world inflation have provoked influential calls from 'supply-side' economists in the USA in recent years to revive it.

GRADUALISM: The policy proposition that changes in the rate of growth of the money supply should be engineered by the central bank at a slow and steady, not a sharp, pace of change.

INCOME-CONSTRAINED PROCESS: A process of adjustment in which the capability of individuals to adjust is limited by their current income-earning power.

IS-LM ANALYSIS: In 1937 J. R. Hicks published what was to be a highly influential interpretation of *The General Theory* which summarised the differences between Keynes and the classics in terms of two curves describing the workings of the goods and monetary sectors of the economy—the IS and LM curves (Investment-Savings and Liquidity-Money) respectively. Hicks actually labelled them the SI and LL curves, but, following Alvin Hansen's (American) textbook, it is the former notation which generations of economics students recognise.

KEYNESIAN COUNTER-REVOLUTION: An interpretation of Keynes's *General Theory* that arose in the 1950s and 1960s and which re-integrated his message into the body of neo-classical economic analysis.

LIQUIDITY PREFERENCE: The demand to hold immediate liquid command over resources—in other words, the demand for money. Keynesian theory assumes the demand for money is determined by the level of (real) income, the level of nominal interest rates, and by (possibly unstable) expectations in the minds of speculators.

LIQUIDITY TRAP: A Keynesian hypothesis that situations exist in which the demand for money is infinitely elastic with respect to the nominal rate of interest. Under such conditions, any increase in the money supply will simply be 'soaked up' by financial asset holders who want to sell bonds to get into money. Even an expansive monetary policy would be unable to depress the rate of interest (and thus stimulate investment demand). Empirical research in monetary economics has failed to reveal the existence of a liquidity trap for any time-period, including the years of the inter-war depression.

MARGINAL EFFICIENCY OF CAPITAL (MEC): The rate of return over cost yielded from additional investment of the most profitable type available.

MARGINAL PROPENSITY TO CONSUME (MPC): The change in aggregate consumption caused by a change in national income.

MARGINAL PROPENSITY TO SAVE (MPS): The change in aggregate savings caused by a change in national income. The MPS is the 'mirror-image' of the MPC, as MPS and MPC add up to unity.

MONETARY ECONOMY: An economic system in which goods are not directly traded against each other (as in a barter economy), but are traded for money at agreed money prices.

MONEY (STOCK, or SUPPLY, OF): Money is anything that is used as a medium of exchange. Thus the stock or supply of money includes not only money issued by the central bank, but also conventional monies, e.g., the deposits of commercial banks that are used for the purpose of making payments.

MONEY ILLUSION: The belief or perception that the money or nominal magnitude of something (e.g., wages) is the same as the real value of it.

MONETARISM: The modernised form of the quantity theory of money. The central propositions of monetarism are that variations in the level of nominal economic activity are determined primarily by variations in the stock of money; and that whilst the initial impact of changes in the stock of money affect real output and employment, eventually the rate of monetary growth affects the rate of inflation.

MULTIPLIER: The ultimate increase in real national income resulting from an increased injection of so-called 'autonomous' expenditure into the economy. It was an hypothesis of Keynes that in a depression the value of the multiplier was greater than unity: an increase in government spending would boost real national income by more than the size of the initial injection. In the simplest Keynesian models, the size of the multiplier is determined by the MPS; in fact it is the reciprocal of the MPS.

NATURAL RATE OF UNEMPLOYMENT: The equilibrium rate of unemployment in the economy, determined by the real forces and frictions embedded in the economy, such as government-imposed minimum wage laws, rent controls, barriers to labour mobility, and the degree and extent of trade union monopoly power.

NEUTRALITY (OF MONEY): The classical proposition that a change in the stock of money will (once it has fully worked its way through the system) eventually change only the general level of prices, leaving all real variables unchanged in magnitude.

NEW MICRO-ECONOMICS OF UNEMPLOYMENT AND INFLATION: A new branch of economic analysis that emerged in the late-1960s and which sought to understand unemployment and the dynamics of wage movements on the plausible assumption that the relevant market information is costly to acquire.

NOMINAL VARIABLES: Economic magnitudes (such as money or nominal GDP) measured in terms of their monetary value. *See* also REAL VARIABLES.

NON-ACCELERATING INFLATION RATE OF UNEMPLOYMENT (NAIRU): *See* NATURAL RATE OF UNEMPLOYMENT.

PERMANENT INCOME: Real income expected in the long run. It is to be contrasted with current income—the income generated in the current time-period, which will reflect transient payments and windfall gains and losses.

PHILLIPS CURVE: In 1957 Professor A. W. Phillips found that there appeared to be a negative, curvilinear relationship between the rate of wage inflation and the level of unemployment, over a century of British economic history. Others subsequently generalised the idea of the Phillips curve to the proposition that there is a stable, negative trade-off between the rate of price inflation and the rate of unemployment (or the deviation of aggregate output from its trend rate of growth).

PIGOU EFFECT (also known as the REAL BALANCE EFFECT): In *The General Theory* Keynes accepted in passing that the volume of real balances—the purchasing power of the stock of money in the economy—would positively affect the level of consumer spending, but went on to ignore it. This presumed relationship, known as the Pigou effect, became the central component of the long post-war debate in economics over the validity of Keynes's proposition that the economy could remain in under-full-employment equilibrium *even with* full flexibility of wages and prices. It was eventually shown that, if a Pigou effect existed, this could not be a valid theorem. *See* KEYNESIAN COUNTER-REVOLUTION and DISEQUILIBRIUM PROCESS.

PUBLIC CHOICE: The name given to that branch of economic analysis which deals with the economics of political and collective behaviour, including that of governments, voters, interest groups, and the bureaucracy.

REAL RATE OF INTEREST: The nominal rate of interest adjusted to account for the rate of inflation (or deflation) of the general level of prices anticipated by borrowers and lenders.

REAL VARIABLES: These include quantities—such as employment and output—and nominal magnitudes *adjusted* for changes in the price level, such as the real rate of interest, and the quantity of real balances (*see* PIGOU EFFECT).

SAVINGS FUNCTION: The relationship between the volume of savings in the economy and its presumed determinants. Keynesian theory assumes that the primary determinant of savings is current income, as savings are, by definition, income minus consumption (*see* CONSUMPTION FUNCTION). Later theories argued that permanent income, income over the life-cycle, or wealth were the more relevant determining variables (*see* other Glossary entries).

SAVINGS RATIO: *See* APS.

STAGFLATION: The concatenation of rising inflation and rising unemployment. The phenomenon of stagflation is inconsistent with the idea of a stable, unshifting Phillips curve trade-off between inflation and unemployment.

TARGET RATE OF UNEMPLOYMENT: The measured rate of unemployment at which a government aims in its macro-economic policy.

QUANTITY THEORY OF MONEY: The theory that movements in the general level of prices are determined by the amount of money in circulation in relation to the real aggregate supply of goods and services. Keynes asserted the quantity theory to be wrong in *The General Theory*, since it ignored variations in the demand for money arising from motives for holding money for other than transactions purposes. The modern, reformulated quantity theory takes this criticism on board and allows that variations in the velocity of circulation of money may also determine the course of the price level.

WEALTH: The discounted value of an income stream receivable in the future. Wealth is thus a *stock* concept, whereas income is a flow over time.

HOBART PAPERBACKS in print